EXPLORING
THE FEN-EDGE

Also by Rex Sly:

From Punt to Plough

Fenland Families

Soil in their Souls

First published in 2017
© Rex Sly
www.rexslyinthefens.com

Book design by Megan Sheer
sheerdesignandtypesetting.com

Printed by Jellyfish Solutions Ltd.

ISBN 978-1-909811-41-6

EXPLORING
THE FEN-EDGE

ALONG THE ROMAN CAR DYKE

REX SLY

THE FEN-EDGE

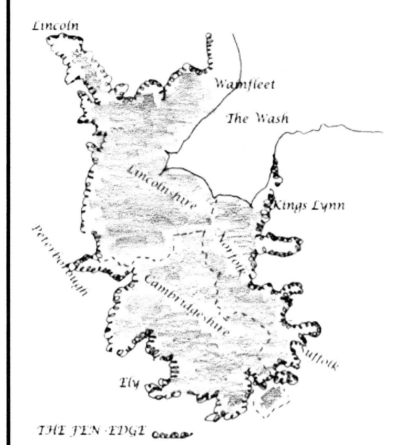

Lincoln

Wainfleet

The Wash

Lincolnshire

Kings Lynn

Peterborough

Norfolk

Cambridgeshire

Suffolk

Ely

THE FEN-EDGE

The Fens
of Lincolnshire
Cambridgeshire
Norfolk & Suffolk

Separating the fens from the uplands is the fen-edge – not a defined area as such, but a divide between the uplands and fenland. It could be defined as 'lying in ming', an area of no defined boundary – a chartered surveyors' term used in the past when many such areas existed in the fens. The counties of Lincolnshire, Cambridgeshire, Suffolk and Norfolk all lay claim to their areas of fen and so include fen-edge in their domain.

Having written on the fen interior, I felt a wish to explore this area, which is part of the fenland landmass and, in many ways, has been missed out by travel writers of the past.

Before mankind stemmed the tides with sluices and other tidal barriers, saline waters from the sea would have reached the fen-edge via the many rivers passing through the fens. The fen-edge itself was at one time vulnerable to the vagaries of nature, especially from the upland rivers surging through the fen-edge on their way to the Wash. An old adage was, 'letting live water into the fens', meaning flowing waters. Great forests existed on the fen-edge thousands of years ago, but due to climate change and rising sea levels they were submerged to decompose, forming the peat soils we know today. This phenomenon occurred on the fenland side of the fen – the edges, which were and still are the lowest parts of the fens. Many meres existed in these low-lying areas of fen prior to drainage during the 19th century, with the advent of steam-driven pumps.

There is evidence of human settlements here as far back as Mesolithic times, particularly along the fen-edges. Bronze Age evidence has been found on the fen-edge south of Peterborough on the black fen. Many Iron Age salt workings are evident between the Deepings and Billinghay, while Roman and Saxon evidence is abundant.

Glacial activity is evident along the fen-edge, where large deposits of aggregates have been extracted, while further in the uplands limestone, sandstone and phosphates have been mined since the Neolithic period. The fen-edge at its upper reaches is bordered by heathland lying on chalk and limestone substrata. Early settlers lived in these areas and ventured into the fens for fishing, fowling, and grazing their livestock during the summer months.

There is no straight line dividing the fen from the uplands. Small upland peninsulas run into the fens and conversely the fen creeps into the uplands, as if both have vied for their common rights against evolution. Many early settlements off the fen had grazing rights on common pastures in the fens. They could also take fish and wildfowl from the fen meres and lakes and had the right to dig turves from the peatlands for burning in their settlements. Drainage Acts in the late 18th and early 19th centuries brought to an end villagers' rights to the commons when all lands were enclosed. Some commoners retained their rights, but most of the enclosed land went to the families who financed the drainage itself. Productivity of the newly drained land increased, as did the demand for labour to work it, with many villages and towns doubling their population over a very short period.

Up until the First World War, pastoral agriculture was the main farming enterprise on the fen-edge. This changed mainly to arable cropping during the two World Wars and has remained as such to the present day.

My journey begins at Eye near Peterborough, following the route of the Car Dyke to Lincoln, running between these two great cathedral cities. The Car Dyke is 57 miles long, believed to be of Roman origin, and follows the fen-edge along most of its course but deviates deeper into the fen in some parts.

I may occasionally stray up off the fen-edge onto the higher ground, which I will refer to as uplands. I will also delve into the fens themselves, back into my homeland – or anywhere my curiosity takes me.

KEY TO SYMBOLS IN THE TEXT

 Point at which a walk is suggested

 Specific reference to the Car Dyke

The places described in this book are covered by
the OS Landranger map sheets 121, 130, 142.

THE FEN-EDGE

PETERBOROUGH TO BOURNE

As I approach Peterborough on the A16 from Crowland, my introduction to the fen-edge is the very impressive Bowstring Bridge (240 feet long). Engineers constructed a raised approach to the bridge, which carries you up above the fen to cross the Roman Car Dyke.

Whoever cut the Car Dyke would have been proud of this bridge, which spans their great legacy to the fens. Many millions of pounds were spent on the bridge in order to preserve a very small part of the Dyke itself, signifying its historic importance to fenland history in marking the divide between fen and uplands: the fen-edge.

The Bowstring Bridge spanning the Car Dyke at Eye

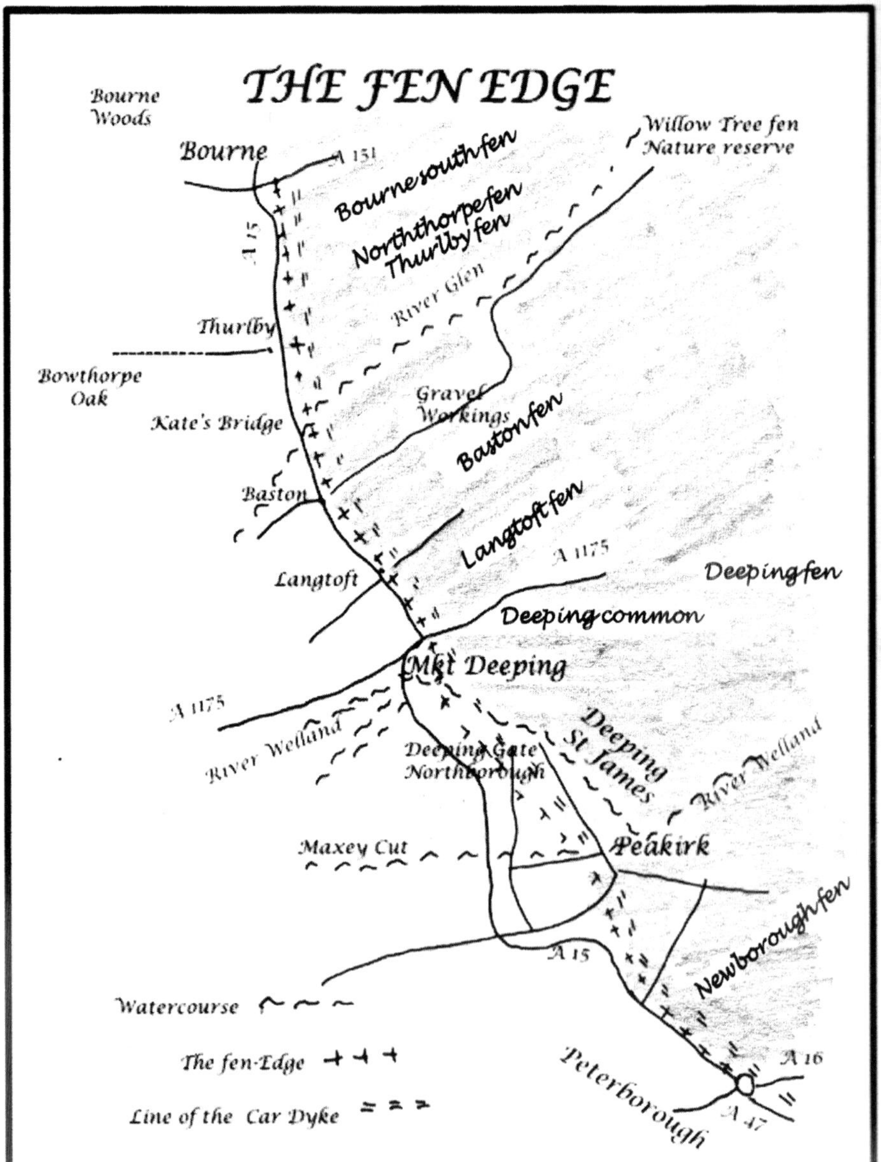

THE FEN EDGE

The Fen Edge
Peterborough
to Bourne

I will refer to the Car Dyke as Roman, simply because the fen people call it Roman, and since no one has proved otherwise to me it remains of Roman origin. It is claimed by some historians that it was used for the transport of goods for the Roman armies, especially as the fens were major producers of salt from the sea. Others say it was used as a drainage system to gather water coming down into the fens and steer it to the rivers, a catchwater drain, seen on other parts of the fen-edge. Some even suggest it could have been a boundary separating ancient tribes – but all that is conjecture. The reader, like me, will have to ponder over its origin, and speculate on it purpose. It baffles our archeological experts and confuses our historians, so who am I to come up with an answer? It is without doubt one of the greatest feats of ancient linear engineering in the UK and yet defeats the experts as to its origin and purpose.

HISTORIANS' COMMENTS ON THE CAR DYKE

Miller and Skertchly, in *The Fenland Past & Present* (1878), were convinced that the Car Dyke extended from Ramsey to Lincoln. They also mention that William Stukely (1687–1765), an English antiquarian born in the fens at Holbeach, suggested the Car Dyke started at Cambridge. Cambridgeshire CC on one of their websites give examples of the Car Dyke at Cottenham, Landbeach and Waterbeach.

The importance of the Car Dyke from Peterborough to Lincoln was evident from the fact that seven forts were erected along its route to guard it, at Northborough, Braceborough, Billingborough, Garrick, Walcot, Linwood and Washingborough. There is, though, very little evidence of these forts along its course – yet another mystery surrounding the Car Dyke. So many unanswered questions surround it.

Whatever the answers are, I intend to enjoy exploring it, standing on its banks and just maybe imagining who its engineers were, who used it and for what purpose.

Not all historians in the past were convinced that it was of Roman origin. Dugdale only a has a brief mention of it in Norfolk 'that the back dike from Narborough bars to Cardike be kept in breadth 8 feet and in depth 5 feet'. Wheeler's

The Car Dyke from Fen Bridge, Newborough Fen

History of the Fens in South Lincolnshire has only a brief mention of it, and Rawnsley refers to the Roman 'Carr Dyke' at times as a catchwater, and sometimes as a navigation channel.

The Car Dyke is one of the least known of our ancient monuments, with only one area of it, at Potterhanworth, a designated Site of Special Scientific Interest, or SSSI. There are other sites along its route designated Sites of Nature Conservation Importance (SNCIs), at Branston Booth Pits, Burnt Wood, Bottom Barff, Nocton Wood, Metheringham Barff, Blankney Wood, Blankney Car Dyke Hayfield, Car Dyke Bank, Car Dyke Bank (southeast of farm), Martin Wood, North Kyme Common (North Kyme End), and Park Wood. White in his *Directory of Lincolnshire 1882* mentions several villages on the Car Dyke as being 'near the Car Dyke Navigation'.

There have been many references to the Car Dyke in the past but not a single book had been published devoted entirely to this ancient monument, until Heritage Lincolnshire published their detailed report in 1979, *The Lincolnshire Car Dyke*, followed by a booklet on the Car Dyke in 2006. Even after extensive research and excavations along its course, its authors Brian Simmons and Paul Cope-Faulkner still came up with no conclusive evidence of its origin and purpose.

After crossing the Bowstring Bridge I turned left at the roundabout, then first left at the next one brought me to a spot to park and I set off along the dyke towards the bridge. It is a fine example of the dyke here and still used as a catchwater drain, evident by the flow of water along it. This section of the Car Dyke is a particularly good example of its purpose, as a catchwater drain or canal or both, with the towpath on the fen side, and the raised bank to prevent floodwater spilling into the fen. I also followed it south into the village of Eye for a short distance, where it is still being used to carry water, but not to the extent it does downstream.

I took the A15 signed to Sleaford following the edge of Peterborough city until the Werrington roundabout where I turned off to go into the fen. Almost immediately after I turned off the A15 I crossed a stone bridge over the Car Dyke. This bridge is Fen Bridge, Grade II listed, late 18th century. The bridge is built entirely of stone and on the skew, allowing the bridge to cross the dyke at an angle. The voussoirs and keystone are stone blocks which have been shaped, while the rest of the bridge is stone as quarried.

I walked along this stretch of the Car Dyke upstream to an identical bridge called Gunton's Bridge.

The Car Dyke is large, well embanked and probably as it was when the Romans cut this drain.

Whether it will remain so with urban development drawing closer to it, remains to be seen, but hopefully, like the construction of the Bowstring Bridge further upstream, this fine example of the Dyke will remain for future generations to witness.

Guntons Bridge: Simon Gunton (1609–76) was the vicar of St John's in Peterborough and the Prebentry and sub-treasurer of the cathedral in 1646. He wrote *The History of the Church of Peterborough* in 1686, which has been reproduced by facsimile, and in which my family is mentioned. He did much for the cathedral, one such deed being to recover chapter land given away by Henry VIII and to hand it back to its rightful owners. The bridge that carries Gunton's name has not been preserved in the same condition as the Fen Bridge, even though both are listed. I believe, where possible, all bridges should have a name linking them with a person or a connection with some event in our history. Should we not give the Bowstring Bridge I crossed earlier a name, for sadly it is anonymous? Maybe Car Dyke Bridge would be a fitting name, since it is only there because the present generation chose to preserve a small part of such an ancient monument our forefathers chose to neglect.

Leaving the bridge along the fen road I noticed the change in soils, from mineral soils containing particles of stone, sand or gravel, to the more organic fen, made up of silt, clay and peat.

My OS map marks an area to the west as 'Milking Nook', a cluster of houses, and so my curiosity draws me across to it. It is flat arable land now, but before the enclosures it was what was known as a common. Some villages and settlements had their own individual commons, exclusive for the villagers to graze their livestock on. Where several villages shared rights to one common, that was known as intercommoning rights. These villages had the grazing rights for summer grazing and would have driven the cattle along their own droves and gates to the common. Individual commons had different rights and laws as to what could and should not be adhered to. Many commons were enclosed in the 17th century through to the 18th century, the last ones in the 19th century.

The road across the Newborough Fen comes out on the Thorney to Peakirk road where an old inn stands called The Decoy. Like many country inns it has changed hands many times in my time and one wonders if it will survive or fall to the fate of so many similar inns today. Let us hope in the future some traveller like me will still record its existence. The soil around here is organic, and like all fenland peat soils is depleting annually. It would be interesting to know what a travel writer will see in a century's time …

On the other side of the Thorney–Peakirk road in Borough Fen I could see the duck decoy surrounded by a large group of trees. Duck decoys were used to catch live ducks. They consisted of a pond with star-shaped channels, usually eight, leading from the pond and tapering to a point – these were known as pipes. The pipes were covered in nets which led into cages at the points. Along the pipes were a line of high reed-screens set along the water's edge. A dog, or

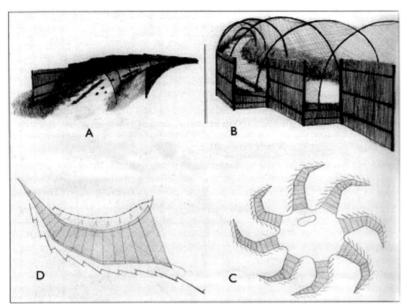

A plan of a duck decoy

A: *The pipe covered with netted frames leading from the pond where the ducks are enticed down from the pond by the dog.*
B: *The screens and dog leaps behind which the man and dog work.*
C: *Typical decoy pond showing pipes leading off.*
D: *Diagram of pipe.*

piper as they were known, usually a similar colour to a fox, under the guidance of the decoy man enticed the ducks from the pond down the pipes and towards the net cages.

Borough Fen Decoy was the last commercial working decoy in the UK, until 1951. It is now used by The Wildlife Trust for ringing waterfowl; it is open to groups through the Borough Fen Parish Council between April and July. There were once hundreds of similar decoys across the fens, mainly during the 18th and 19th centuries before most of the fen was drained. Billy Williams, the last decoy man, is buried in Peakirk Church. His family ran the decoy from 1670 to 1958 when he died. Many farms in the fens still have the name Decoy Farm.

Travelling along the Thorney road towards Peakirk, on the left I notice Nook Lane and a warning sign depicting a cow crossing. Not all things have changed since the enclosure of the common, because just opposite the sign is a livestock farm – at times there must be a need to cross the road when driving cattle to and from their fields at Milking Nook.

MEETING THE UPLAND WATERS

On the approach to Peakirk the road rises as you come to the village. Like most fen villages it stands on higher ground than the surrounding fen.

Having a passion for drains and pumps, I turned right just before the bridge and level crossing, signed to Sissions Farm. The track follows the Folly River to the pumping station which discharges into the River Welland.

The Folly River runs from the Car Dyke north of Borough Bridge up to the Welland at Peakirk. Whether it was originally cut when the Car Dyke was, or at a later date, I am unsure. Dugdale's 1772 map of the area names it as 'The Drain'.

Peakirk is an important drainage location on the fen-edge, having the Maxey Cut, the River Welland, the Folly River and the South Drain all converging here. Upland watercourses passing through the fen-edge are managed by the Environment Agency (EA), and watercourses below the 5 metre Ordnance Datum Newlyn (ODN) contour line are managed by the Internal Drainage Boards (IDBs) across the fens.

This is a good place to park and walk along the River Welland bank into the fen, as I did that day. The bank goes all the way to Crowland, and was created in the 17th century as a flood defence between the Welland and the low-lying fens on its eastern side.

If you walk towards Crowland on the bank, on your left is the start of Crowland Washes which were constructed by Vermuyden, a Dutch engineer, in the 17th century as overspill reservoirs. In times of heavy rain when the river was full to capacity, excess floodwater would spill into these washes where it remained until the river levels dropped, then was released back into the river on its way to the sea.

Upstream of Crowland are the Cowbit Washes which served the same purpose as Crowland Washes, all taking floodwater from the River Welland.

After the 1947 floods the Coronation Channel was cut round Spalding, which has prevented both washes from flooding since then – but who knows what the future may bring. Similar flood washes were constructed in the fens during the

The Maxey Cut joins the River Welland at Peakirk

same period, such as Whittlesey Washes along the River Nene and the Hundred Foot Washes along the River Great Ouse.

Weather permitting, the walk from Peakirk to Crowland is a place for solitude and a feeling of unrestricted space, especially when the cloud formations are in harmony with the weather. You will also pass close to the decoy on the right, evident by the tall trees surrounding it, which stands out like an oasis on the bleak fen.

I remember being at the pumps at Peakirk in April 1998 after a great deluge of water came down from the uplands and which coincided with heavy rains in the fens. The Welland overtopped into Cowbit Washes just north of Crowland, not seen since the floods of 1947. It was a testing time for the EA and the IDBs, but they coped. It was nature reminding us of the perils she can inflict, when she chooses to!

This is a part of the fens I love to walk along and it can be very exciting if the Maxey Cut and the Welland are in full flow. It was this converging point of water carriers at Peakirk that inspired Sir Peter Scott to set up the Peakirk Wildlife Trust reserve in 1946. Although it closed in 2001, parts of it can still be seen on the edge of the village leading out to Deeping Gate.

Peakirk village centre

PEAKIRK

Peakirk derives its name from the Norse, *Pega-Kirkja*. The village itself is truly fen-edge, being neither fen nor upland – evident by the stone houses from the past sitting alongside later brick houses like those seen in the fens.

I intend to visit many churches on my travels along the fen-edge, and in fact I will not have to travel far from one to another. St Pega was my first church to visit. Having neither tower nor spire it was not easy to locate, but I eventually found it near the war memorial, set in among mature trees.

CHURCH OF ST PEGA

I was told that St Pega founded a cell or nunnery here in 716 to the east of the present church. She was the sister of St Guthlac, the founder of Crowland Abbey. In 1016 King Edmund Ironside issued a charter giving land to build a place of worship in the village.

The church of St Pega is built of local Barnack stone in mostly Decorated English and Perpendicular styles, with some parts dating back a thousand years. It's a quaint little church and while it has no tower it does have a bellcote supporting three bells at the west end of the nave, north and south aisles, with clerestories along the nave.

The church was open when I called and the tall, narrow nave gives you the impression of entering a great hall. The 15th-century chancel is impressive for such a small church, with Perpendicular mullion windows. There is a door with a Norman arch on the north aisle. I do not know if it is true but I was told that a door on the north side of a church is known as 'the devil's door'. Legend has it that they were left open at baptisms to allow the child's evil spirits to leave. They were also used for processions at the same service, and at funerals.

The door in the porch is especially fine, with beautiful ornate carvings on the spandrels above the door, known as a tympanum, and characteristic of Norman and Gothic buildings. The small windows in the clerestories restrict light into the nave, which makes the 13th-century murals on the north wall only just visible if the lights are not on. An ancient wooden screen separates the north aisle from the nave, and worthy of note is the reading desk, over 600 years old, set on a pedestal in the shape of eight clustered wooden columns placed on stone. Reading desks were used prior to lecterns, which came into use in the 15th/16th centuries and up to the present day, usually depicting an eagle or pelican.

I felt elated that the first church I entered on my travels might be the oldest I would visit, but who knows what lies ahead along the fen-edge? I am not an expert on church architecture – my knowledge comes from a few note-books I have on the subject.

The village has an inn called The Ruddy Duck. I have frequented it for too many decades to remember, with fond memories. It is still very popular locally and for travellers from around.

The Hermitage is on the right-hand side of the road as you leave the village towards the Deepings. It is a private house now but the chapel adjoining the house can be seen from the road. The Hermitage Chapel was built in 1470, and restored in 1880 by Abbot John de Wysbech, so a villager told me.

I often use *The Fenland Past & Present* (1878) by Miller and Skertchly for my research. My copy has an inscription in it which reads 'this book to be given to the community of the Holy Trinity on the death of Lilian M James, December 19th 1950'. I purchased it from the Sue Ryder secondhand bookshop in Spalding after the Hermitage closed.

I looked for evidence of the Car Dyke here, but found none around the village, although I was told excavations suggest it came to where the village is today.

After leaving the village going towards the Deepings I crossed a bridge over the South Drain, and then turned left along a narrow road. As I drove down the

The tympanum above the door in the Church of St Pega, Peakirk

road two embankments stood out: on the left is the South Drain and on the right is the Maxey Cut.

The Maxey Cut was cut and embanked in the 1950s as a relief channel for the River Welland, following the disastrous flood of 1947 which I witnessed as a young boy. This area is very low-lying and was prone to flooding before 1947 but the two water carriers have proved successful since the 1950s. The line of the Car Dyke crossed

Spire of Glinton Church from the North Drain

somewhere along this road, so I stopped to try to find it. Sometimes, especially in the spring when the soils are void of crops and dry, crop marks can be seen. The 1806 OS map shows the Car Dyke crossing the road where the bridleway crosses, going right to the Maxey Cut and left to the bridleway leading to Glinton. The soil on either side of the road is not fen but mineral, evident by its colour and gravel content.

The tall spire of Glinton Church glints in the sun and draws me down the bridleway to a stone bridge which crosses the South Drain. A peaceful spot to sit and ponder is on the bridge, where there is an information board mentioning the poet John Clare who loved this spire. The spire is 140 feet tall, and is said to be taller than the tower it stands on, a formidable landmark on the fen-edge. Back in 2004 British Telecom planned to erect a telephone mast in the middle of the village of Glinton. Many villagers were concerned that it would conflict with the beauty of the church spire and so wrote a letter to the Chief Executive of BT, Ben Verwaayan. They included John Clare's poem on the spire, and after reading the poem BT decided not to go ahead with the mast.

GLINTON SPIRE

Glinton, thy taper spire predominates
over the landscape and the mind
musing the pleasing picture contemplates
like elegance of beauty much refined
by taste that almost defies and elevates
once admiration making common things
around it glow with beauty not their own.
Thus all around the earth superior things
those struggling trees though lonely seem not lone
states it was given to the those struggling trees though lonely seem not lone
but in thy presence wear superior power
and e'en each mossed and melancholy stone,
gleaning cold memories round oblivion's bower
seems types of fair eternity - and hire
a lease from fame by thy enchanting spire

As I approached the B1143 main road I noticed a stone bridge at the end of that road and parked to get a closer look. This area is called The Nine Bridges, denoting its past history. The road was at one time the only link between The Deepings and Peterborough, forming a vital link between the two, but susceptible to flooding along this stretch. I parked at Nine Bridges to take a look at its fourteen continuous arches.

The Maxey Cut only carries water when the Welland is in flood, which it was that day. It is quite a sight to see the floodwater pouring through the arches of the bridge. While looking spectacular to the human eye, the colour of the water denotes the loss of topsoil, something I fear for the future of our farmland.

During the spring flood of 1998 I stood on Crowland Bridge watching the brown water pouring under the bridge. I went home and put my thoughts into a poem.

Nine Bridges between Glinton and Northborough

COLOURED WATER

I stood on Crowland Bridge today
and watched the water in dismay,
a river swollen running brown
sediment from field and town;
Brooks overflowing with banks awash
gathering soils – so someone's loss,
pipes and drains will do their job
and drain the land beneath the sod.

Into dykes the pipes will run
for a purpose not for fun,
flowing water brown and black
off to the sea no turning back;
This blend of nature from past years
I watch go by with mournful tears,
millenniums of nature's toil
a gift to us – it was that soil.

Lodes and leams carrying water fast
transporting soils from the past,
a blend of clays and silts and peat
flow down our drains cut so neat.
These are the soils that we do farm
and did inherit free from harm,
but man's quest for food and living space
are words he says before his grace.

Via estuaries to the Wash it flows
and then to where no one knows,
my tears fall on waters dark
visions of the future stark.
And so off to Fosdyke if I can
to wave farewell to soils lost to man,
they served my ancestors as well as me
now lost to us and gone to sea.

John Clare witnessed dramatic changes in the countryside, which grieved him, but each generation witnesses one kind of destruction or another, human or material.

There are many interesting places to walk around this area, especially when the Maxey Cut is in flood.

NORTHBOROUGH

Joining the A1143 road and wishing to turn right towards Northborough was difficult, so I turned left and found a safe place to turn around. Approaching Northborough as I entered the village on the bend, I noticed a large medieval stone gatehouse. It is the entrance to the Manor, which dates back to 1340 and is said to have been built by Geoffrey de la Mare. When Lord Orford made his sailing voyage around the fens in 1774, one of his associates, Mr Farrington, took a horse and carriage from the Nene at Peterborough to Spalding races. On this journey he recalls passing a building 'which appeared to be an ancient monastery, or building dedicated to religious purpose'. He did not enquire its purpose, but regretted doing so. To me it sounds like this manor.

Oliver Cromwell's widow moved here after her husband died and lived with her daughter, Mrs Elizabeth Claypole. She died in 1665 and is interred inside the church, as is her daughter.

Left: *The Pack Horse inn, Northborough*. Right: *The Manor, Northborough*

I parked near The Pack Horse inn, an inn of long standing and with an excellent reputation today. Walking into the village I passed stone houses, some of which are thatched – a blend of stone from the uplands and reed or straw from the fen – neither fen nor upland, but truly fen-edge.

CHURCH OF ST ANDREW

The church stands out in the village, a fine stone structure in various styles but mainly Decorated English and Perpendicular. It consists of the nave with clerestories, 13th-century north and south aisles, 14th-century chancel, south transept and a porch. The west end of the nave is Norman and has a bellcote with two bells.

The chancel is a fine structure of Early English design with battlements, and two stair turrets with pinnacles and finials of floral design with fine mullion windows. The church is interesting in its different periods of church architecture.

It is coincidence that the first two churches I visit on my journey have no towers but bellcotes on their naves. The two bells here were cast in 1410 and 1611 respectively, the latter by Tobias Norris of Stamford. His premises are still in Stamford where the ancient inn The Toby Norris stands – recommend it, I will

indeed. The church was locked, as many are today, but I read that inside is the tomb of Elizabeth, daughter of Oliver Cromwell, who lived in the Manor.

On the north corner of the chancel outside I found the headstone of John Clare's wife Martha, who was buried here in 1871. John was born in the nearby village of Helpston, the son of a farm labourer, and he died in the Northampton General lunatic asylum. I do feel if any poet in history can be associated with the fen-edge it has to have been John Clare. He was born and lived much of his life on the fen-edge at a period in history when it was witnessing dramatic changes. The countryside ran in his genes and in his writings, which he emblazoned with local dialect and detail of what he saw and felt was happening around him at that time. It was the time of industrialisation, enclosures and men leaving the land for jobs in the cities and towns. He witnessed and wrote about the fen and the enclosure of Helpston Common. Helpston is only a few miles to the east of Peakirk, where his cottage has been transformed into a visitor centre, café, museum, and a collection of some of his works – well worth a visit (www.clarecottage.org).

DEEPING GATE

Leaving Northborough I headed for Deeping Gate and crossed the River Welland into Deeping St James. The link between the two Deepings is a fine stone bridge spanning the river. The word 'gate' is common in the fens, usually describing a road: Broadgate, Fengate, Outgate, and many more. Its origins are Nordic, and mean a track, road or byway, frequently associated with access to and from the commons. It is also found in cities, towns and villages, such as Queensgate in Peterborough and Castlegate in Lincoln, which are now street names.

Where possible I like to walk over a bridge, so I parked my vehicle and strolled onto the bridge and watched the upland waters glide through the stone arches.

The Bell inn stands within yards of the bridge in Deeping St James – a welcoming sight to travellers entering the village. In *White's Directory of Lincolnshire of 1842*, The Bell inn is mentioned along with ten other inns and taverns in this village. If that was not enough to quench the villagers' thirst there were seven beer houses as well.

The bridge is believed to have been built around the early 19th century. Gervoise, in his *Ancient Bridges of Mid and Eastern England*, written in 1932, writes 'the bridge is scarcely more than a century old'. The three arches are segmental and almost semicircular in design, the centre one being built of brick while the two outer arches are of stone. The voussoirs are also stone and consist of triple arch rings built in three orders, as are often found in bridges built in the 17th century. The road is 13 feet wide with recesses over the four cutwaters. It has a stone dated 1651, which was from the original bridge and reset, as well as a stone on the north buttress dated 1880 to commemorate the great flood of that year which destroyed many bridges in the fens. It is a Grade II listed structure.

The bridge over the River Welland at Deeping Gate

In the reign of James I at the General Session of Sewers held in Stamford in 1620, the River Welland was to be cleaned and twelve navigational locks were to be built between Stamford Town and East Deeping (Deeping St James), a distance of nine and a half miles. The river fell into disrepair during the 18th century and two schemes were put before the Sessions in 1810 by Thomas Telford and Mr Brown to repair the locks and improve the river, but were not carried out. There were many problems in maintaining rivers during this period due to their management being in the hands of several bodies, which so often could not or would not work together. This situation remained until the Land Drainage Act of 1930 when the river catchment boards were brought into being to manage the rivers from their source to the outfalls. Some work was carried out downstream of this bridge in 1740 when John Grundy of Spalding, and Humphrey Smith, built new locks, which remained in regular use until the 1870s; relics can still be seen downstream of this bridge. It was the advent of the railways that brought about the demise of the barge traffic on the river. After crossing the river I was in Deeping St James.

DEEPING ST JAMES

The river is beautiful at this point both up and down stream, with some pleasant walks along it.

Edmund Waterton, a noted antiquary, moved to Waterton Hall (later to become Deeping Manor) in Deeping St James from Yorkshire in 1879. It came into the occupation of the Catholic order of Xaverian Brothers as a novitiate in 1919. During the Second World War the Xaverian preparatory school moved from Sussex to Deeping Manor for safety reasons, but after a fire in the Manor in 1945 the school moved back to Sussex. Two of my brothers went there in the 1940s, as did many local Catholic and non-Catholic boys. The Manor is no longer there.

Waterton was a devout Catholic and gave land for a Catholic chapel to be built near the Manor; the chapel remains as part of a private house. A new Catholic church was built in the last few years, very modern and appreciated by the local Catholic community who worship there.

I walked upstream to one of my regular watering holes, The Waterton Arms. I am not sure if it was built by the family or renamed after an existing inn since it was not mentioned as The Waterton Arms in *White's Directory 1882*. All my life it has been renowned for its fine ales and food, much of the food being sourced locally. Just past The Waterton Arms there is a sign for Priory Hall, where a path leads to the church.

CHURCH OF ST JAMES

The church's impressive size derives from its early days as part of a Benedictine priory, which was dissolved in 1539. The fine tower at the west end of the nave, rebuilt in the 18th century, has a spire and balustrade. The porch is 13th century and there are many fine windows in the church.

The nave is most interesting, having seven bays of Norman arches on the south side with a triforium in the clerestories. The north side of the nave has no aisle but does have three large Perpendicular windows dating from 1408. There are wooden pews along the nave and south aisle with elegant bench ends. The tub font with a cover is from the Norman period.

The nave ceiling is a tie-beam structure supporting a flat white painted ceiling. The ceiling on the nave and the chancel does not reflect the grandeur of this church; I wonder if, when the tower came down, it damaged the roof and this ceiling was a replacement. The chancel was re-roofed in 1830 and I presume the ceiling was rebuilt at the same time.

One curiosity which interested me was the graveside shelter used to protect the vicar from northeast winds from across the fens. I have seen another in Pinchbeck Church near Spalding but never witnessed one being used at a burial – and I have witnessed inclement weather at several fen funerals.

Left: *The nave in the Church of St James.* Right: *The village lockup, Deeping St James*

My lasting impression of the church was looking at up at the triforium supported by the beautiful Norman arches, illuminated by the sun streaming through the aisle windows.

Near the church is a stone building with slate roof on which is a bellcote, with one bell. I believe it was a girls' school built by the vicar in 1851.

About a hundred yards south of the church on a fork in the road is the remains of a cross, which was also the village lockup. The cross was built in the 15th century, probably as a market cross. In 1819 it was converted to an overnight lockup for up to three felons, who remained there until being taken to the magistrate the next day.

There is no boundary between Deeping St James and Market Deeping; the years of urban development have wedded them together. Deeping St James has always supported a larger population than Market Deeping but has no town centre as such. The rise and fall of the populations in both are reflected in the influences of local agriculture:

Deeping St James population:
1801 – 1,160; 1841 – 1,733; 1881 – 1,648; 1921 – 1,544; 2015 – 6,923

Market Deeping population:
1801 – 803; 1841 – 1,219; 1881 – 1,212; 1911 – 966; 2015 – 6,200.

In 1801 an act of parliament was passed to enclose 34,000 acres in Deeping Fen and the surrounding area. Agriculture prospered until around 1860/70, helped by steam-driven drainage pumps, dredgers and the railways to transport goods onto and off the farms to markets. Cheap imports of food from around the world then forced agriculture into the worst depression in its history, up until the First World War. There was an exodus of labour from the land into the towns and cities.

MARKET DEEPING

Market Deeping has a spacious town centre with shops, inns and many fine stone buildings. When strolling along its streets it is difficult to believe you have one foot in the fens; it has an aura of an upland town, but is fen-edge by descent.

The River Welland flows down through Leicestershire, passing through the town of Stamford. Before the age of railways it was a navigable link between Spalding, then a port, and Stamford, with much barge traffic through the town. The Deeping Stage, once a coaching inn, has not lost its old character. The entrance where coaches once passed through to the stables is enclosed and now serves as a dining area. It is a favourite of mine when visiting the town.

The town centre of Market Deeping

There are here two of the best award-winning fish and chip shops in this part of the country: The Boundary, and Linfords. Linfords is in the centre of town, The Boundary between the town and Deeping St James. The fens have always been a gourmet's delight for fish and chips, stemming from the wonderful potatoes grown on fen soil and fish from the port of Grimsby in the days when it was one of the largest fishing ports for landing cod in the UK.

Market Deeping is a pleasant town to stroll around, the centre having the appearance of a once thriving market town on the fen-edge, and the buildings a relic from those past days. The river adds to the charm of the town, flowing through it and winding its way on to Deeping St James and then to Peakirk. I could not resist standing on the town bridge, a stone three-arch structure built in 1841 at a cost of £8,000 – a vast sum in its day.

After crossing the bridge from the town I had time for a stroll along the riverside. On this side of the river you can see the gardens running down to the river and the rear of The Deeping Stage, up to the old locks, where I crossed the river. There is no longer any barge traffic on the river, but the Deepings' annual raft race is held here annually in July, along with various festivities.

CHURCH OF ST GUTHLAC

The church is 13th century, of Early English Perpendicular style. Built of stone, it has a three-stage tower on the west end of the nave, with a parapet, clock but no spire. There is a sundial on the south side with the inscription 'The Day is Thine', and another on the north side with the inscription 'The Night Cometh'.

The nave has north and south aisles with clerestories, and a chancel on the east end of the nave, along with a 13th-century porch on the south aisle. Inside, the nave has an arcade of semicircular Norman arches on the north side, and pointed arches on the south side, and there are some fine stained-glass windows in the church. Wooden bench pews line the nave, with various carvings contained in a circle on the ends. The font is of the Perpendicular period.

On my journey from the Deepings along the fen-edge I will be passing many villages on the way to Lincoln. Almost all have one thing in common: they all have their own individual fen named after them. Before the enclosures of common lands the villagers would have had grazing rights in the fens, and some would have had rights to take fish, eels and fowl from the lakes and meres. From the peatlands they would have dug turves for fuel and cut sedge from the mere beds. Fen-edge villages often shared their rights with other villages deep in the fens themselves. These villages situated just above the fen relied on the fen for their very existence.

Many drainage schemes were carried out in the 17th century across the fens, causing them to shrink and induce flooding. The engineers at that time did not carry out improvements to the river outfalls restricting the flow of water from the newly drained fens into the Wash. In fact the drainage deteriorated, leaving 'the fens in turmoil'. During the 19th century the advent of steam-powered excavators enabled the river outfalls to be improved, and helped the fens to be drained once again.

It was wealthy individuals who financed the drainage schemes – names such as Lord Burleigh, the Earl of Linsey, Earl Fitzwilliam, along with certain adventurers and others of substance in these areas. These families then became the owners of the land that was drained and enclosed in the 19th century. The fen-edge villages had always relied heavily on the fen for their livelihood before the enclosures, and even after they were drained many took to farming the drained fens, as tenants. Today these enclosed areas can be easily identified by their vast emptiness, being sparsely populated with farmsteads and cottages.

The upland commons were cleared of scrub and woods and then divided up into fields enclosed by hedges and lines of trees. The fenland enclosures were divided up into fields by the cutting of delphs, dykes, drains and cuts, to drain the land. These also served as boundaries to the fields, being void of hedges and trees.

The font in the Church of St Guthlac, Market Deeping

In the early days after the enclosures, much of the farm work was carried out by gangs of labourers who travelled down into the fen to work. The work was known as 'piece work', which meant that they were paid for what they did by the 'piece of work', such as picking potatoes by the acre or ton, or singling sugar beet by the acre. Even thatching stacks of corn would be done in this way, each stack being a 'piece'. Dykes would be mown or cleaned by the chain. This way of working carried on until machines replaced manpower in the mid to late 20th century.

After leaving Market Deeping the first village I came to was the village of Langtoft.

LANGTOFT

As I entered the village it was heartening to see that The Wagon & Horses inn was still in business – it is mentioned in *White's Directory 1842*.

On the fen side of Langtoft, extensive gravel extraction has been carried out in the past two centuries and is still going on today. There are also extensive gravel workings, from past and present, on the east side of the village stretching out to Tallington.

The course of the Car Dyke lies on the fen side of the village, but I found no evidence of it. Langtoft Common was enclosed in 1792, the fen allotments in 1801, and by 1881 the fen commons were all well drained and part of Deeping Fen.

I find the fluctuation in rural village population numbers interesting, and try to read into the reason for such fluctuations. Taking Langtoft as an example, the village population figures I found are as follows:

1801 – 386; 1841 –778; 1881 –584; 1922 –496; 1933 –470; 2011 – 2000+.

The rise from 1801 to 1841, an increase of over 100%, could be attributed to the increase in arable land requiring more labour as a result of the drainage of the commons. By 1881 the population had declined to 584, which could have been due to the great agricultural depression which began around 1870 and lasted until 1914, when labour left the land to find work in the cities. The population decreased again to 496 by 1922, maybe due to losses during the First World War. By 1933 it had decreased slightly to 470, almost back to its early 19th-century figure. The late 1930s was also a period of agricultural depression until the Second World War.

CHURCH OF ST MICHAEL AND ALL ANGELS

The church dates from the 13th to 15th centuries and is built of coursed and squared limestone rubble and ashlar. The tower is at the west end of the north aisle with a spire, clock, and five bells. The nave has clerestories above the north and south aisles, and a chancel.

The church was locked when I made a visit, which was a disappointment. I had read that the nave ceiling was a wooden tie-beam structure with heads of men and women look down from the ceiling.

The village houses and buildings are built mostly of brick with some stone ones scattered along the streets. The Wagon and Horses inn is on the main road at the crossroads, looking very neat and inviting, but sadly closed when I passed it.

The Wagon and Horses inn with the Church of St Michael and All Angels in the background in Langtoft

BASTON

The village of Baston is also characteristically fen-edge, having a mix of stone and brick houses, though mainly of brick. There are two inns, The White Horse and The Baskervilles.

Population (*White's 1882*): 1801 – 457; 1881 – 763; 2011 – 1,469.

The increase from 1801 to 1881 was as a consequence of the drainage of Deeping Fen. Unlike neighbouring villages where the population was declining by 1880, Baston did not. There were extensive gravel extraction works nearby, which may have kept the labour force in work when men were deserting the farms in nearby villages.

CHURCH OF ST JOHN THE BAPTIST

The church stands alongside the main street, having a square tower with parapets, four decorated pinnacles on each corner, and a clock. It is 13th/14th century but has been restored over many years.

The nave has north and south aisles, the porch being on the south. The chancel looks to be later than the rest of the church. Unusual features are a bellcote on the west end of the south aisle and an ancient porch on the south aisle with a sundial on its apex roof.

The church was open when I made my visit, with groups of schoolchildren being taught on religious matters by the vicar and their teachers. This was so encouraging to witness, and I did not wish to interfere with their lessons. However,

I did see a plaque on a wall, which caught my eye. It was in memory of Isabella Mary Garfit, daughter of George Richards Denshire Esq of Thetford House, who died, age 2, in 1846. Only a few hours before, I had been to see Mark Richardson who lives at Thetford House, an ancient house on the site of a village that no longer exists, but it is mentioned in several antiquarian books. It is also on the side of the Car Dyke where a spring feeds it, which then runs into the River Glen. Mark had said the Denshires had emigrated to Australia.

White's 1842 mentions the family at Thetford House, but there is no mention of them in *White's 1882*, so I presume the family emigrated between those dates. Between 1870 and 1914 British agriculture suffered its worst depression in its history due to foreign imports undermining home-produced goods. At this time many tenant farmers and landowners left the land. On the main street I found the old chapel, built in 1877, now converted to a motor garage with a showroom adjacent. In the showroom I saw some excellently restored classic cars – one especially took my eye, a Jaguar XK150.

I found the seating figures of both the church and the chapel in *Kellys 1922 Directory of Lincolnshire* interesting, the church seating 340 persons and the chapel 300 – almost an equal divide between the Anglican church and non-conformists in the parish.

The old Methodist chapel in Baston converted to a motor garage

INTO THE FEN

While at the village of Baston I drove down into the fen, where large developments of gravel extraction can be seen. Early extractions were left to flood; some have been transformed into wildlife areas and some for fishing. Also of interest are the more recent sites, which have been reinstated to farmland on a lower plain, mostly over the past few decades.

Beyond the gravel workings the soils change from a mineral content to black peat soils over a very short distance. I carried on through some of the black peat soils to the Baston Fen Nature Reserve, which is managed by the Lincolnshire Wildlife Trust (LWT).

This is an ideal place to walk along the River Glen bank, either upstream or down. Upstream is a convergence of several watercourses, notably the Bourn Eau that was once a navigable link between Bourne town and the River Glen. It is very noticeable how much higher the River Glen is than the surrounding land due to land shrinkage, the river being embanked.

Gravel workings and reinstated works restored back to farmland

Willow Tree Fen Nature Reserve at Tongue End

Further along the road towards Pode Hole is the Willow Tree Fen Nature Reserve, also managed by the LWT, consisting of 100 acres of recently restored wetland from arable farmland. I did not walk on the reserve that day but have done so before and always enjoyed the wildlife, and peace.

After a good walk along the river bank or in the Willow Tree Fen Reserve, The White Horse near the church in Baston village is an ideal place to replenish your calories in friendly surroundings. It is owned by local farmer Mark Richardson who sources much of the food from his own farms, or from neighbouring farmers. The family is a long-standing farming family in this area, and enthusiastic conservationists, owning part of the Car Dyke which they have preserved. It is refreshing to see a country inn revitalised and thriving when so many are closing around us. I may add that the Richardson family have always enjoyed a good pint, or two, themselves.

KATE'S BRIDGE – HISTORICAL INTEREST

My next stop was just up the road at Kate's Bridge. I had been here several times in the past to look at the bridge and always enjoy seeing it again.

After Baston, still on the A15, I came to Kate's Bridge, an important fen-edge site for several reasons. The east and west Rivers Glen join together to the west of the A15, passing through here as one watercourse. It then travels through the fen, eventually discharging its waters into the River Welland at Surfleet Seas End. The Car Dyke runs close by the bridge; the Roman road of Kings Dyke as well as Kings Street Drain are here, all under the name of Kate's Bridge, a meeting point of history.

There are many natural springs along this route, which are fed from the limestone aquifers to the west. I remember the farms around Baston supplying an abundance of watercress up until the 1960s, and where the Waterside Garden Centre now stands was a watercress farm. Today the same water supply is used for irrigating agricultural and horticultural crops.

From *Lincolnshire Place Names* the earliest record of Kate's Bridge is 'Catebrigg' (1245, 1276, 1295) or 'Katebrigg' (1275), possibly originally old Norse *Kati's Bryg*, after a person's name. We have on record, in the 14th century, a bridge known as Kate Brigg where the present one stands over the River Glen. There were several Commissions around the 1320s suggesting improvements to the River Glen. One such Commission in 1323, held in Thetford, reported that 'all the ditches and banks, from Kate Brigg in Kesteven unto the sea in Holand,

The old listed Kate's Bridge over the River Glen

A section of the Car Dyke near Kate's Bridge on private land

were broken on each side, and did then stand in need of repair; that is to say — to be raised higher by 2ft. and thicker by 12ft.; and that the towns of Thurlby, Obthorpe, and Eyethorpe, lying to the north side of Kate Brigg, ought at their own proper charges, to repair, dig and cleanse the same; and from the said Cross to Abbottescot, on the side the town of Brunne [Bourne].'

It is said that there was once an ancient village nearby; the names of Thetford, Thurlby and Obthorpe are found close to the bridge but Eyethorpe is not. Thetford is a farmstead and house nearby.

Kate's Bridge is a Grade II listed structure. It is late 18th century, made of ashlar. It has a single elliptical arch with rusticated voussoirs flanked by pilasters. Above a plain band to the low-coped parapet on the west the keystone has a female carved head, presumably 'Kate'. There is also the former road bridge here, now bypassed just a few yards away.

While there I strolled east beside the River Glen, along a path known as The Macmillan Way, one of the great footpaths in the fens. It stretches from Boston in Lincolnshire to Barmouth on the west coast of in Wales, a distance of 280 miles. A short distance along the path a section of the Car Dyke can be seen running southeast up to Thetford House where it is spring-fed. However, it is on private land.

THURLBY

Thurlby lies mainly on the west side of the A15 but I turned right near The Five Bells inn to visit the church. The last time I was at the church was to attend the funeral of a friend who was a close friend of my son, so I thought I must visit again to pay my respects. The church has a fine set of new gates repaired in 2002. I saw that one of the benefactors was Nigel Cooke, whose funeral I attended, and this made my visit worthwhile. Thurlby Fen was enclosed in 1810, as were neighbouring fens.

CHURCH OF ST FIRMAN

The church stands overlooking the fens, with a small dyke close to the church which I was told was the Car Dyke. If that is so, I am surprised the church was built so close to it.

The church is of Norman and Early English styles. The tower on the west end of the nave is Norman with crucifixes at the finials on the spire. It is unusual in that it has twelve gabled niches on the spire and four on the tower, enabling the five bells to ring out across the fen-edge. The north and south aisles both have porches; the chancel has transepts and the nave has clerestories. Sadly the church was locked when I visited, as I would have liked to see inside. I had read that the two transepts were used as chapels, with interesting piscinas and hagioscopes and some oak screen-work in the church. The font also would have interested me, as it is a cylindrical shape of Norman period. There is a cut mark at the base of the tower.

The church is part of the Ness Group, along with Baston and Langtoft. As a point of interest, W.J. Rawnsley (*Lincolnshire Highways & Byways 1914*) mentions that the best preserved stretch of the Car Dyke is near Thurlby. I could only find a very small part of the dyke remaining, alongside the church.

INTO THE UPLANDS

MANTHORPE

Having planted many trees in my lifetime, especially on my birthdays, this passion led me to Manthorpe village to the west of Thurlby. I had read there was an old oak tree believed to be around 1,300 years old, with a girth of over 40 feet, at nearby Bowthorpe Park Farm. The farm is said to be the site of a village which stood there many centuries ago. Its disappearance may have been due to the Black Death when many villages were razed to the ground, but I have no evidence that was the case.

I passed through Manthorpe to join the A6121 towards Stamford and found the entrance to the farm a short distance on the left-hand side along the road.

White's 1842 mentions 'the hollow trunk of a venerable oak, in which fifteen persons might sit at a table, the girth being 45 feet'. The oak was in full leaf when I saw it, a majestic sight, and I am sure it would look even more majestic in its autumn coat and also without its leaves; without its leaves it would show off its gnarled trunk.

Around the Bowthorpe Park oak tree has grown a fun farm, opened this year. This is a new venture for the family with minimal catering facilities, and parking in wonderful open countryside. There are cattle, sheep of various breeds and goats to interest the children as well as fun games. Parents can enjoy the surrounds, especially the old oak. When I made a visit it was busy, many people looking at the oak, some admiring the livestock, and some doing nothing more than lying on the grass and experiencing the tranquil countryside. The Blanchard family of all ages were there to chat and look after the visitors – truly a family enterprise.

The family is the fifth generation to live there working the soil, which consists of heavy clay in the lower fields and with a high mineral content of limestone on the higher land. Prior to the Second World War much of the farm was grassland, but due to compulsory orders during the war, most of the grassland was converted to arable farming. Richard Blanchard manages the farm and is gradually putting the clock back three-quarters of a century and laying more fields down to grass, to

The Bowthorpe Park oak tree

enable the family to build up their beef cattle enterprise. The family is passionate about their livestock and their soil structure, and farming a system that suits their soils, for future generations of Blanchards to come. My last book title was *Soil in Their Souls*, a title befitting to Richard (www.bowthorpeparkfarm.co.uk).

Returning to the A15 and travelling towards Bourne I passed Math Wood and Elsea Wood, both interesting ancient woodlands, and accessible to the public (www.thisisbourne.co.uk).

BOURNE

Entering the town I could not help but notice the development which has occurred in recent years, both urban and commercial, eating up the fen-edge.

Bourne population:
1851 – 3,717; 1871 – 3,850; 1881 – 3,760; 1911 – 4,343; 1911 – 13,961.

The figures show that the population was fairly static between 1851 and 1881, had slightly increased by 1911 but has grown since then, mainly in the past three decades.

Almost in the centre of the town are the Wellhead Gardens on South Street, a pleasant introduction to the town itself, and a reminder of its origin. Bourne, once spelt 'Bourn', derives its name from the Anglo-Saxon meaning water or stream.

Walking into the gardens along the path leading up to the war memorial are 22 crosses and plaques on both sides of the pathway. The plaques depict the various regiments the soldiers fought in during the Second World War, their names being inscribed on the memorial itself. When I walked around the gardens it was a bright late winter's morning, being enjoyed by parents with children feeding the ducks, a good place to walk and relax.

The Red Hall is close by. It is thought to have been built in 1620, a stunning Grade II legacy building, which was used as a railway ticket booking office between 1890 and 1959. Twice during that period it came close to demolition, but thankfully it was saved, and today is worth a visit. Opposite the park is the church which has several interesting old features, with a stream flowing alongside the church.

The town centre still retains its origins as a spacious market town. The Corn Exchange building is still there, but the livestock market that was once behind it is now a supermarket and shopping centre. I remember it as it once was: buzzing on a market day, the men in the market, the Corn Exchange or the inns, while the wives came to shop. However, the town is still a busy place with its shopping centre, hotels, inns and cafés around the centre.

Left: *The Well Head Gardens, Bourne.* Centre: *The Red Hall, Bourne.* Right: *Bourne town centre*

Bryan Browning, a Lincolnshire architect, designed the Sessions House. A plaque on The Exeter Arms in the centre of the town marks the birthplace of William Cecil, Lord Burleigh KG, Lord High Treasurer of Queen Elizabeth I, born 13 September 1520. Another plaque on the building names Frederic Manning 1882–1935, Australian author and poet who wrote his First World War novel *The Middle Parts of Fortune* while living here at the former Bull Hotel in 1929; the hero was named Bourne. Bourne Eau, on the fen side of town, ran from the town to the River Glen at Tongue End, a navigable link with Surfleet and on into the Wash or upstream to Spalding.

The town was also the home of Raymond Mays, who developed British Racing Motors (BRM). Between 1950 and 1977 the team started in 197 Grands Prix, with 17 victories, 11 pole positions, 15 fastest laps, 1 Drivers' World Championship and 1 Constructors' World Championship. Graham Hill's 1962 World Championship was the first time a British driver had won the World Championship in a British car. Peter Gethin's 1971 Italian Grand Prix victory at Monza was the fastest Grand Prix of the 20th century, at an average speed of 151 mph.

The date 7 October 2012 is a day I will remember for a long time: it was BRM Day in Bourne. The town was closed to all traffic and many BRM and other racing cars were paraded in the town (I am not allowed to say 'raced' around the streets). Damon Hill, the son of Graham Hill, and Jackie Stuart were just two of the drivers that day, and many racing cars from the past were on display. The sounds, smell and sights were spectacular, as was the whole atmosphere in the town – let's hope we see it again before too long. There is a memorial to Raymond Mays on the roadside of South Street alongside the Wellhead Gardens.

CHURCH OF ST PETER AND ST PAUL

This ancient church includes many periods and styles of ecclesiastical architecture. It was once the site of Bourne Abbey, which was established in 1138 by the Augustinian order but dissolved during the Reformation.

The tower is at the west end of the church, at the end of the south aisle. It has pinnacles on each corner, each with a weather vane, a clock facing south, and it accommodates six bells. At one time there were two towers, which is evident by

the flat structure along the west end of the church. The north aisle has clerestories and a porch on the aisle. The south aisle has a vestry on the side with a sundial on the exterior. The nave is large and lofty with the chancel on the east end, with fine stained glass set in stone mullion windows above the altar. Four Norman stone-arched pillars line the nave, with a 15th-century stone font standing at the west end of the nave and an ornate stone and marble pulpit along with an ornate brass lectern at the chancel end.

Impressive tower arches overshadow the bell-ringers' stations, plain wooden bench pews line the nave, and there are choir stalls in the chancel. The ceiling is wood of tie-beam construction and not as old as much of the church. During the 19th century there was much restoration and this ceiling may date from that period.

The church is well lit, the clerestories allowing ample light into the church, which is reflected off the nave and aisle walls, which are painted white. It had a warm, welcoming feeling about it as I walked in. The church adds splendour to the town and it's well worth spending some time here, just browsing and meditating. The stream running past the west end adds to its charm.

At the edge of the cemetery is an old school building and former playground, in need of restoration. It was most probably the site of the original grammar school, founded in 1636 and funded by Thomas Trollope, 2nd Lord of the Manor Bourne Abbots. The roof looks as if it was once covered by thatch.

The last time I was in the church was once again at a friend's funeral. I suppose living in the same area all my life, as my ancestors have done we create friendships spread over a large part of the fens, and beyond. Some might call it insular or parochial; I call it a bond of friendship with like-minded people.

Church of St Peter and St Paul, Bourne

THE CAR DYKE IN BOURNE

While in the town I was curious to see if I could still find traces of the Car Dyke, which my maps told me passed through the town as we know it today. Coming in on the A15 from Thurlby, at the first roundabout I took the fourth turning to the Lidl superstore. I found the Car Dyke at the rear of the store, alongside the car park. It does not look like a Roman channel now, just a drainage channel which most people seeing it would say was another fen dyke – but it is still there to be seen. There is a footpath shown on my OS map between Bourne and Thurlby along the Car Dyke which I did not walk, but hopefully will one day.

I had seen an old photo from the mid-20th century of the Car Dyke on East-gate near The Anchor inn where it joined the Bourne Eau, so I went there in the hope that some of it remained. Sure enough it was there as the photo had shown, with crystal-clear water running along it past The Anchor, which is still in business but was closed when I took my photos. I thought it extraordinary to find two small sections of the Car Dyke in the town after so much development had taken place there.

In contrast to the walk in the town, Bourne Woods are ideal for a casual stroll to see some fen-edge countryside. It is ancient woodland with mixed conifers and semi-natural broadleaf trees with ponds. There is a car park and picnic area but no toilets. Cyclists are welcome but only on hard paths. Fauna and flora abound depending on the season.

Presumed to be the Car Dyke where it met the Bourn Eau

BOURNE TO
BILLINGBOROUGH

My map of the Car Dyke shows it running from Bourne to the village of Dyke and sure enough I found it a short way down the first road off to the left, bordered by houses. Further towards Dyke the road is open countryside on both sides, fen soil on one side, fen-edge soil on the other.

After a short distance I saw a small brick tower in the centre of open fields. It is a breeding place for barn owls. Len Pick, a local farmer who died in 2004, endowed the Len Pick Trust with the surrounding farmland, and on it was a barn, the home to generations of barn owls. The Trust's old farm buildings were demolished, with some of the materials being used to build the tower. Since the Trust was formed, hedges and trees have been planted to create conservation areas in the surrounding fields. Such a wonderful legacy for Len to be remembered by and enjoyed by people and nature.

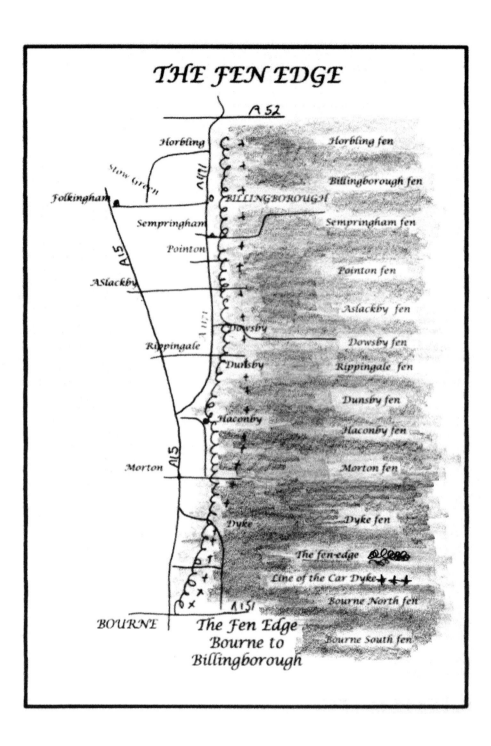

THE FEN EDGE

The Fen Edge
Bourne to
Billingborough

DYKE

The village of Dyke stands between the 5 and 10 metre contour lines, with the Car Dyke running through it, which is still evident.

It's a quaint little village with The Wishing Well inn standing prominent and welcoming in the centre. The village has an Eau Well in it, hence the name of the inn. The well is on the small green in the centre of the village alongside the village sign. It was empty of water when I made my visit; more than likely it has been capped off as many of the springs have been along the fen-edge.

Adjacent to the inn are the remains of a windmill, which has been carefully preserved. Dyke also has its own fen, Dyke Fen, which runs down to the South Forty Foot Drain.

Most of the villages I have passed through from the Deepings to Bourne are slightly lower than the 10 metre contour, while the villages I will be passing through from Dyke to Billingborough are on or above the 10 metre line. When these fens were enclosed in the 17th/18th centuries – and some as late as the 19th century – the watercourses all led towards the centre of this landmass, feeding into the rivers and main artificial drains before finally discharging into the Wash.

The inquisitive traveller could journey down into the fens from almost any of the roads between Bourne and Billingborough. The roads, like the watercourses, all lead to the South Forty Foot Drain where the water finds its way to Boston to be discharged, either by gravity or pumps depending on the flow, into the Witham estuary. The South Forty Foot Drain was cut in 1757, improved in 1846, and during the 1960s many pumps were installed to drain the fens on either side.

When exploring the fens I often take a sandwich with me and park somewhere on a fen road, usually near a watercourse, for a moment's solitude. I have tried in many countries and places to experience total silence, which is not easy to find, for often nature can be just as noisy as urban sounds.

MORTON

After leaving Dyke I joined the A15, heading north for Morton. Leaving the A15 to turn into Morton village, I noticed that The Lord Nelson inn was closed and boarded up. On the opposite side of the road was The King's Head which burnt down a few years ago – a great meeting place for many of us in our younger days. It is sad how the village populations have grown considerably and yet there are fewer and fewer watering holes left, although once they were the hub of village life.

The church is the focal point of the village, standing upright on a mound where the road forks to either side, left to Haconby and right to Morton Fen. The Five Bells inn is beside the church and nearby, painted white, is the quaint old church hall. This street shows the village's character, with Morton Grange behind a medieval stone wall, a large square 18th-century house opposite and a smattering of old houses and barns, some of which have been converted to dwellings. Further down the village on the fen road I was surprised how much development has taken place, including a new school. Not far down the fen road I found the Car Dyke and also a sign 'Car Dyke Farm'. The Car Dyke here was really only a small fen dyke.

Morton church hall

CHURCH OF ST JOHN THE BAPTIST

The church is of cruciform design with the nave, north and south aisles on the west side of the tower, and the large chancel on the east side. It has a magnificent clock and tall pinnacles on each corner of the tower, which also has a stair turret on the outside of the southeast corner. A tall nave with clerestories in the north and south aisles dominates the west end of the church.

Entrance to the church is via a porch at the west end of the nave, which I found interesting. Iron gates set in a stone arch enclose the entrance, stone mullion windows on either side of the porch make it light inside, and the solid oak door into the church with a smaller door set in it, known as a wicket door, invites you into this fine church.

Inside, the nave has four Perpendicular stone arches with a hammer beam wooden roof. A south transept on the tower contains a priest's door. There is a cut mark near the priest's door on the outside wall.

In 1861/62 extensive improvements were carried out in the church, including new wooden pews, pulpit and reading desk restored, and most of the stained-glass windows inserted. The cost was £2,000, a huge amount by today's values, the benefactor being a resident landowner, which reflects the prosperity of farming in and around Morton in those days. The chancel was re-roofed, and the east end rebuilt at the same time, along with stained-glass windows installed in memory of the Arden family. The chancel ceiling is wooden hammer beam, the walls white, making it light and airy inside. It also contains some interesting features such as a three-seated sedilia and a piscine.

As I entered the church the 15th-century stone font caught my eye; if only it could speak, I would be an avid listener, and wish it many baptisms in the future. I was lucky that this lovely church was open and to be welcomed inside to join in prayers, which were being said at the time.

Church of St John the Baptist, Morton

Nave in the Church of St John the Baptist, Morton

HACONBY

It's a pleasant ride over to Haconby through neat well-farmed countryside, where there are still a few grass fields, denoting some mixed farming, and some substantial farmhouses in and around the village. With the advent of larger farming units, many of the old traditional farmhouses have been sold off. The village has retained its inn The Hare and Hounds, a quaint building with pantile roof, dormer windows and a welcoming sign 'Open all day Saturday and Sunday'. There is a small green in the centre of the old part of the village, which could have enhanced the village if planners had thought of retaining some of its former charm; sadly the same has happened to many other villages.

I did drive a short way down the fen and found some remains of the Car Dyke, still there but not its former self. I was sorry I did not find a better example of the Dyke but I am pleased I did go down the fen road because the sight of the church steeple from there was remarkable.

CHURCH OF ST ANDREW

The church stands on the edge of the village, overlooking some neat rural countryside. It consists of an imposing square tower with a tall spire, which has four pinnacles on the corners. The spire was struck by lightning on 7 July 1877 but thankfully was repaired, and it still towers above the fen and fen-edge.

The wicket gate to the Church of St Andrew, Haconby

The nave has clerestories on both sides with north and south aisles, and a large chancel on the east end of the nave with a porch on the north aisle, which appears to be little used. The entrance to the church seems to be through a door on the north aisle. The tower is large and square, constructed in layers of cut stone filled in between with uncut stone, which is rather unusual.

There is a small wicket gate which opens onto a footpath leading into open fields via a kissing gate. I thought how much more rural could you get for a church entrance; it was a welcoming entrance for country folk, depicting a union between the church and the countryside. Maybe in the past the village folk entered through the north entrance and the rural folk came from across the fields through the wicket gate to the south porch? As I left I recognised some of the names on older gravestones, families still farming on the fen-edge and in the fen itself. There is a rather nice old manor house near the church.

The road between Haconby and Dunsby rises above the fen, with several woods in the distance. Between Bourne and Aslackby to the west of the fen-edge on a higher ridge of land there are some large remnants of ancient woodland, a complete contrast to the stark fenland landscape void of ancient woodland. That is not to say there was never any woodland in the fen. Thousands of years ago there were many forests on the fen side of the fen-edge, which were destroyed by rising sea levels and then decomposed. These areas can be identified today where the fen soil is black and peaty, and ancient bog oaks appear out of the soil. The peat soils have depleted over the past century due to erosion and arable agriculture, but bog oaks do still appear occasionally.

Bourne Woods west of Bourne, Callans Wood northwest of Stainfield, and Temple Wood above Kirkby Underwood are owned by the Forestry Commission and accessible to the public. The other woods are mainly privately owned.

Driving to Dunsby village from the A15, Dunsby Wood caught my attention. I remember this area in the 1970s, when on either side the road hedges were all trimmed by hand enclosing grass fields with wonderful beef cattle grazing in them; today most of the fields are arable.

DUNSBY

My first introduction to Dunsby as I approached the village was the church, in a prominent position almost on the road, positioned to catch your eye and draw you into the church itself. Entering the village I noticed several houses of varying size and uniform design, with an agricultural estate air about it. I knew that, like Morton, it had been a rich farming area for several generations. This is evident by some large houses, probably of 19th-century period and maybe earlier; one especially I noticed with some fine Wellingtonia trees along its drive. These are extremely fine trees from America which always catch my eye when travelling. It became fashionable in the mid to late 19th century to plant them in the gardens of substantial houses in the countryside. Many still remain from this era, even though the houses they graced may have been demolished. Back in time these larger houses would have been occupied by people known as yeoman farmers.

Unlike Morton, where stone houses were prominent, the houses in Dunsby were mostly built of red brick. *Kellys 1922 Directory of Lincolnshire* states that 'the soil is rich loam, gravel subsoil, chief crops being wheat, oats, barley, peas and roots'. Today's cropping would be wheat, oilseed rape (OSR), beans and spring barley, crops described as 'combinable', meaning that they are all harvested with a combine harvester.

Until recently the cropping would have consisted of winter wheat and OSR, but due to this close rotation an injurious weed known as black grass has swept across the entire country. The weed has become unmanageable, compelling farmers to extend their rotation to include spring crops, and leaving the land bare from harvest to the spring in an attempt to eradicate the black grass during that period of fallow, then drilling in the spring. During the Second World War close rotation of crops also caused problems, with certain crops causing a build-up of eelworm in the soil. Now we are suffering a similar problem with close rotation of crops. Farming economics have brought this about, at the expense of good husbandry. When I went to agricultural college in the late 1950s, my father said to me, 'Learn the technical and theoretical side of farming, but do not forget how to farm'; by those words he meant 'good husbandry'.

CHURCH OF ALL SAINTS

The church has a square embattled tower and is built in three stages. A niche on the west side of the tower has the figure of Our Lord, and there is a cut mark at the base of the tower. The nave has clerestories with north and south aisles, with the chancel on the east end of the nave. The south aisle is the length of the nave with a porch, whereas the north aisle extends beyond the nave, creating a vestry.

The church was locked so I could not see inside but I did attend a friend's funeral here recently and admired the interior. I read in *White's Directory 1882* that the bells were sold in 1891 and replaced with a peal of Hanington chimes, no doubt to finance repairs to the church.

Kellys 1922 gives the prominent landowners here as Measures, Caswell, Atkinson Brockton and Wadsley Longstaff, of which Measures, Caswell and Atkinson still farm in the area.

The population has changed little since the 19th century: 1841 – 195; 1881 – 163; 1882 – 223; today less than 150. There has been very little development in the village due I was told to no one wishing to sell land for development. However, I did see a large new house built recently on the edge of the village.

THE DORRINGTONS OF DUNSBY

Driving down the fen road I saw a large herd of dairy cows. Knowing that dairy farms on the fen-edge are few and far between, my curiosity got the better of me. The farm belongs to the Dorrington family who I knew of, but had not met before.

I met Simon who farms with his brother Ross, the third generation to farm here. To keep the family tradition of farming alive, Simon's son Chris has recently joined the team. Hesitant at first, he worked in the city for a few years but the love of the farm drew him home after a refresher course at the Royal Agricultural University in Cirencester. The farm is managed to very high standards using the most up-to-date husbandry and science, but I am sure Chris will make his mark in the future, as farming is always changing.

It was Simon and Ross's grandfather who bought the farm in 1924, moving from Friskney near Skegness. I mentioned to Simon that the village had a certain air about it, with a look of belonging to someone, or somebody with substance. He informed me that the London Charterhouse charity once owned the Dunsby estate consisting of 2,361 acres, along with the village. *White's Directory of Lincolnshire 1842* mentions that they owned most of the soil around the village. The

Simon Dorrington with some of his dairy herd

The Car Dyke in Dunsby Fen

Charterhouse charity built the houses befitting the size of the holdings, in the mid to late 19th century. This would also explain the Wellingtonia trees, which were fashionable in that period. Charterhouse, like many other London charities, had agricultural estates around the fens and fen-edge, and like many other charities sold them after the First World War, Charterhouse selling theirs in 1919. The tenants on the estate bought most of their holdings, the Dorringtons buying their farm from a tenant who had bought it from the estate in 1919.

This farm is, I believe, unique for this area. It is a mixed livestock farm with a wider spread of cropping such as peas, beans, potatoes, cereals and grass leys. This practice of farming declined rapidly after the UK joined the European Economic Community in 1972. The dairy herd of Holsteins numbers over 300. It looked good and well managed, the animals scattered in fields around the farmstead – a scene which has not changed since Simon's father started a milking herd. The day I called, cows were calving in a field near the village, a touching sight for anyone to see.

I drove down the fen road with Simon where he showed me the Car Dyke. This section is managed by the Environment Agency and the Dyke is a fair size, carrying water from the becks which flow off the higher land into the fen, through the fen and on to the South Forty Foot Drain. Well down the fen he also pointed out two springs which run all year from the limestone aquifer below the soil.

Further on down the fen we came to the pumping station on the South Forty Foot Drain which was in operation pumping the water from the two springs into the drain. I have been told since that there are many springs along the fen-edge, which supply water to the Forty Foot Drain. It is causing some concern that water is being wasted when we should be preserving more of it for domestic use.

I noticed a number of fields along the fen road which had not been farmed for several years, but left to run wild, or 'wilding' as the term is now. The owner – not the Dorringtons I might add – obviously chooses not to farm them but relies on his Area Payments, or subsidy from the government, for income. It will be interesting in years to come to see if these fields are in the same state as they are today when we eventually move out of the European Union. I did have to admit to Simon that they were a wonderful haven for wildlife.

INTO THE UPLANDS

RIPPINGALE

Rippingale village does not have a foot in the fen or even a toe, but has its own fen, Rippingale Fen, bordering Dunsby Fen. Many years ago I stood on the bank on the east side of the Forty Foot Drain in Pinchbeck North Fen and watched water running into the drain on a hot, dry summer's day from Rippingale Fen. I though it unusual so I asked a local man standing near me if it was unusual; his reply was 'No, its the Rippingale running drain, which always flows across the fen from up near the village of Rippingale'.

After leaving Dunsby I passed over the beck which feeds the running drain in the fen, before turning up to the village of Rippingale. The Roman road, now the A15, passes on the west side of the village.

White in his *Directory* of 1882 describes the village as 'a large and pleasant village, on a gentle acclivity'. Unsure of the meaning of acclivity I found it means an upward slope. The village stands several metres higher than most of the fen-edge villages I have visited on my journey, still pleasant as White remarked, and tranquil.

CHURCH OF ST ANDREW

The church overlooks the village with The Bull inn close by. The church was open and looked interesting, while The Bull inn also looked interesting but was closed that day.

Sepulchre in the Church of St Andrew, Rippingale

The church is an ancient structure with a fine tower of four stages, topped with battlements and pinnacles on each corner, and a clock. The nave has clerestories on the north side making the church very light inside, and showing off the tie-beam ceiling. The south aisle is divided from the nave by elegant Early English stone arches. There may have been a screen separating the aisle from the chapel; I say that because there is a lovely ornate ancient screen canopy, still in fine condition, below which is an impressive stone pulpit.

White's 1882 mentions that the chancel was restored in 1854, along with renovations to the nave and a new stone pulpit erected in 1856, defrayed by the united donations of Lord Aveland. Lord Aveland was lord of the manor, patron of the benefice and owner of most of the soil.

There are several fine stone mullion windows with stained glass in the nave and south aisle, in memory of prominent families who lived nearby, as well as some interesting ancient tombs. The crossed-legged knights on one tomb are supposed to be Sir Guy and Sir Goband, lords of the manor; the crossed legs are believed to indicate that they were Crusaders of the 14th century. Another tomb is that of Roger de Quincey, a 15th-century knight, with his two wives.

The De Quincey tomb in the Church of St Andrew, Rippingale

I always look at the fonts in a church since that is where most of us have been at the beginning of our life. This one is an elegant stone font, ancient, I would say at least 15th century or maybe earlier. It has witnessed the baptisms of both male and female, rich and poor, strong and weak, humble and great, to go forth into the world before them.

There are many other interesting features I have not mentioned in this church but it's worth visiting to explore them, especially standing behind the font and looking down the south aisle.

Very few village settlements are found below the 5 metre contour in the fen or along the fen-edge itself. Those that do exist came about after the enclosing and draining of such fens and are several miles away from the fen-edge, standing on higher ridges in the fen interior.

Leaving the village I descended on a short journey down towards the fen. Rawnsley travelled this route in 1926 and commented 'as we went on we noticed that the whole of the land eastwards is a desolate and dreary fen, which extends from the

Welland in the south to the Witham near Lincoln'. My eyes saw prosperous farm-steads, newly planted hedges and woods and fields of excellent crops, blue skies pep-pered with satin clouds with birds in the sky.

The period in history that Rawnsley refers to was during an agricultural de-pression when many tenant farmers could not make a living and deserted their holdings. Tracts of agricultural land were just left and became derelict.

DOWSBY

The next village along the fen-edge is Dowsby, a rural village – I say rural as op-posed to farming, which it was many years ago. So few farm workers are needed on the farms today in combinable crop districts, that these villages have become retirement or commuter villages.

As I entered the village I noticed a large house on the left, once a private resi-dence, now a home for the elderly. There are no signs of urban development in the village. Dowsby Hall, an Elizabethan mansion of stone, still stands above the village.

CHURCH OF ST ANDREW

The church has a square stone tower with battlements on the west end of the nave, Early English. It has a nave with north and south aisles with clerestories and south-facing porch, chancel and vestry.

I did not visit the church; in fact it looked lonely and sad, with cultivated land within a few yards of the building. Maybe when I am passing by another time I will have a closer look – I am sure it has something of interest.

INTO THE FEN

DOWSBY FEN

I took the fen road out of the village and where the road bears to the right is the line of the Car Dyke. I have travelled this road many times in the past and always enjoy the open space. Each mile is a step into no-man's land, with Dowsby Fen on my left and Aslackby Fen on my right.

The pumps at the South Forty Foot Drain I remember being built in the 1960s and what a godsend they were to this low-lying fen. Prior to them being installed, they suffered flooding during wet periods. It was at these pumps I saw a dredging barge in the drain. Curious to know what it was, I stopped and spoke to one of the operators, who turned out to be a Dutchman, who told me it was the first time they had used this machine in the UK. The barge sucks the silt from the drain bed and pumps it along a pipe trailing behind it, to a lagoon some three miles down the drain. The lagoons are situated on farmland alongside the drain where the silt settles for a few years and is then spread across the adjoining land.

This method of dredging the drains avoids machines running along the banks, with the silt taken from the drain itself, which eliminates damage to fauna and flora. It causes little disturbance to the watercourse and the wildlife in the drain. It may have been a new method in the UK but the operator said it had been used in Holland for many decades.

Having come this far down the fen I was drawn on even further, to Gosberton Clough. Along the way on the left, between the Forty Foot Drain and the Clough, are some enclosures of the 19th century: the 1st, 2nd, 3rd, 4th and 5th Droves where many small Lincolnshire County Council tenants farm. The fens were at the forefront of a County Council holding movement in the late 19th and 20th centuries. To this day Lincolnshire, Cambridge and Norfolk County Councils still have large land portfolios thanks to pioneers of this movement such as Sir Richard Winfrey,

A Dutch dredger on the Forty Foot Drain

a man born in the fens and who also served as one of its MPs. He is mentioned in more detail in my book *Soil in Their Souls*.

The Forty Foot Drain serves many fens on both its west and east sides. The fens on the west take their names from the fen-edge villages, whereas those on its east side take theirs from the silt-land villages lying in the central fens.

REFLECTIONS

Whatever may be said about the destruction of the wetlands, they were transformed into human habitable areas, to live and farm in, giving those who lived here a decent standard of living. Many lives were transformed, from one of deprivation and squalor, to a healthy and improved standard of wellbeing. I know of many desolate isolated locations where schools were built for the communities which previously had no such amenities. Some buildings still remain, though most are demolished. One site I know, called 'School House Corner', is now just a bend on the River Welland near Crowland. The school had served the families who lived in the fen, now forgotten by most but remembered by some.

However, my journey is supposed to be following the fen-edge, so I crossed back over the Forty Foot Drain and returned to Dowsby. After leaving Dowsby heading to Billingborough I turned left at Millthorpe crossroads. Only a few hundred yards up the incline, I stopped to look across the fens. I have often passed this spot and admired the view across the fens, and so today being a fine day I thought it would be a fitting place to eat my sandwiches.

It is a high vantage point so near the fens. Looking on my OS map it lies just above the 20 metre contour line, in fact at 28 metres. This, for fen man, is truly high country. The view was stunning that day, especially as storms clouds swept across the fens and light reflected off the blades of turbines on a wind farm in the distance.

INTO THE UPLANDS

ASLACKBY

Having time to ponder over my map, I noticed that the fen road at Millthorpe goes down to Aslackby Fen. Unlike most fen-edge villages with a fen to their parish, Aslackby village is some way from its fen, which tempted me to go there.

The village is on the old Roman road, described by *White's 1882* as a 'pleasant scattered village on the banks of a rivulet', and there still is a beck running through the village. There was at one time a castle here, although the only evidence to be seen now is mounds in the field close to the church. The village is quaint, with some substantial houses in it from the past, and some historical prestige. Near the castle was a commandery (the district under a commander) of the Knights Templar, founded in the reign of Richard I by John de Mareschall. When the Knights Templar were disbanded in 1312 the commandery was given to the Knights Hospitaller, until the Reformation. There were remains of the property until the 20th century, but I did not look for remains.

CHURCH OF ST JAMES

The church is in the centre of the village in a prominent position near the green, close to the beck, and well worth a visit. It has a lofty square embattled tower, on which are four pinnacles. Four belfry windows are set in the tower with one holding the clock face. The nave is tall, with large clerestories allowing ample light into the church, and a small spire on the east end enables access to the aisle and nave roof. It has a chancel; north and south aisles line the nave, with the entrance to the church being a south-facing porch. The south aisle has an attractive stone balustrade along its roof. I also noticed a bellcote for a sanctus bell on the east end of the nave roof, but with no bell. It is a beautiful church from the outside and even more so inside, the tall nave giving it a grand presence, especially when standing at either end.

The nave ceiling is a tie-beam ceiling of some age while the chancel, which was rebuilt in 1861, has an arch-braced wooden ceiling. The font is stone, maybe Early English, with a wooden canopy of modern design; there are no pews but rather very comfortable chairs. It was so nice to find the church open, and showing the passing traveller its finery – my thanks to the churchwardens.

As I left the village to continue my journey I could not help but notice The Robin Hood and Little John inn on the A15, it looked so inviting. I had been in it many years ago, and maybe will again.

The beck running through Aslackby village

Left: *The Robin Hood and Little John inn, Aslackby.* Right: *Pointon school*

POINTON

I had read somewhere in my journals of a corrugated iron building where the author was unsure what it was, so I turned into the village to look for it. I found the building in question, and by its appearance it is still used as a house of worship, called 'Christ Church'.

The church was locked at the time so I can only describe the building from the outside. Without demeaning the house of worship, it consists of a main structure with a lean-to on each side, maybe denoting a nave and aisles inside the church, with a porch. It also has a bellcote with one bell.

I have seen similar corrugated iron buildings in New Zealand of similar age, many of which have been refurbished back to their original condition. I hope the same happens to this one, if ever the need arises; it is a part of our national heritage, and just as important as the fine stone churches around. One man told me it was called 'The Tin Tabernacle'.

Nearby is a school built in 1863 at a cost of £500. *White's 1882* mentions it as a large National School attended by around 100 pupils of both sexes, with a small parochial library and a teacher's residence. He again mentions Pointon as being close to the Car Dyke.

Leaving Pointon heading towards Billingborough, I took the road on the left, signed to Sempringham Church.

SEMPRINGHAM

Sempringham was the birthplace of Sir Gilbert de Sempringham, the eldest son of a Norman knight. He took up holy orders and was appointed chaplin to the Bishop of Lincoln, obtaining leave from Pope Eugenius III in 1131 to established a new monastic order. It became known as the Gilbertine Order, consisting of men and women. The monks, following the rules of St Augustine, were known as White Canons, the nuns following the rules of St Benedict. The order was the only indigenous religious order across England. By the time of the Dissolution of the Monasteries there were some 26 houses of varying sizes across the country, the fens cells being established at Cambridge, Fordham and Upwell. There were disreputable rumours concerning their morality, especially being male and female. One rumour I read was of a nun being pregnant by one of the lay brothers who fled when it was revealed. He was captured and brought back to the monastery.

SEMPRINGHAM PRIORY

The last time I visited this site was several years ago. At that time we farmed in Sempringham Fen, at Neslam Farm. Often when going to the farm I took my horsebox with a horse and rode across the fields inspecting the crops – no finer way to get around one's farm. One day I rode to the church, and some distance away I dismounted and walked, leading my horse. I still remember that day; there was something very unworldly and serene around me as I walked up to the church with the horse, who seemed to mirror my feelings. I love this spot just up off the fens, yet within reach of them; it deserves the name fen-edge.

Memorial stone to Princess Gwenllian

The spot where I walked from up to the church now has a memorial stone quarried from Wales. The shape of the stone from the side resembles the silhouette of a veiled nun with head slightly bowed. It was erected there in 2001 in memory of the Princess Gwenllian (1282–1337) who died at Sempringham Priory. Her mother, Eleanor de Montforth, married Prince Llywelyn ap Gruffydd, the last Prince of Wales, in 1278. That glittering ceremony was attended by many royals, including the Scottish King Alexander and England's Norman monarch, Edward I.

Eleanor died giving birth to Gwenllian and being the only child, Gwenllian was perceived to be a threat to the Norman/English Crown. As a consequence she was exiled to the Gilbertine Priory at Sempringham; her father was murdered on the orders of King Edward I of England. She was six months old when taken to the Priory where she remained until her death aged 55. Some 600 years later a memorial cairn was erected in her memory in the 'corner of a foreign field that is forever Wales'. It decayed, being replaced in 2001 with the present stone by the Princess Gwenllian Society. There is a similar stone on the summit of Snowdon commemorating her life.

The view from the church is as rural as one will find in this part of England, with hardly a house or building in sight. I was fortunate on this visit because the key holder just happened to arrive as I was leaving, allowing me to step inside an ancient building.

CHURCH OF ST ANDREW

The church is an imposing stone building, dominated by its large erect Norman tower. The tower is square, with eight delicate pinnacles on it, and divides the nave from the chancel adjoining it on the east end. A north aisle joins the nave and tower; the entrance to the church is via the porch on the south side of the nave. The east end of the chancel is semicircular on its outer wall with an attractive roof to match. Inside, the nave ceiling is wooden, and medieval pews with carved finials with holes at the top to hold candles line the nave; the chancel ceiling is fan-vaulted.

Earl Fortescue was lord of the manor and owned a large estate around Billingborough, which was purchased by the Crown in 1855. Later, around 1870, the Crown re-roofed the nave and built a new chancel. The church holds a very impressive position overlooking the fens and as you approach it from the road, the south view is, I think, spectacular.

There are no remains of the original abbey, which was demolished during the Reformation. It is said that several of the farmhouses on the Crown Estate were built of stone from the abbey.

COMMENT

There are many springs in this part of the fen-edge. Our own farm at Sempringham Fen some two miles from the fen-edge had its own borehole. I remember that it produced the most wonderful clear, cool drinking water in summertime, but it was sealed off in the 1980s. As well as our farm it also supplied a smallholding in the middle of the farm with water. Mr Pearson, a bachelor, lived on the holding with his mother, aged 90 plus, who was extremely healthy and active. She would walk across our fields, then along the hard road twice a week to go shopping in Billingborough. I am sure she would have made 100 and indeed may have done, unless the mains water ended her healthy life when she moved into a home in the village.

INTO THE FEN

Having farmed in Sempringham I felt an impulse to go and see the old farm. Driving along the Neslam road, past Mr Gould's old farm, I came to a sharp bend in the road. I knew there was a grass field just before bend where Mr Gould often grazed his hunters in the summer. I now know this was a medieval site with a moat in it. When the moat was dug it diverted the Car Dyke around the site, but remains of the Dyke can still be seen as a modern drainage channel on the first bend in the road.

Evidence from the Roman and Saxon periods has been found nearby, helping us to believe it is from that period in history.

BILLINGBOROUGH

Having passed through the village most of my life but never having ventured into it, I decided to explore some of it. The centre of the village has an artesian spring whose waters come from the Lincolnshire limestone aquifer to the west of the village. The spring feeds the pond, and can be seen bubbling up from the ground, but it did dry up in the dry years of 1976 and 2001, the only times in living memory. The water is 'chalybeate', meaning it contains salts, which made it an important site supporting Iron Age and Roman settlements. The fen-edge attracted early settlers partly because of the abundance of springs sourcing water from the limestone aquifers, whereas the fens may have had an abundance of water but it was not of drinking quality.

I was led to believe this lack of drinking water in the fens was the reason it had so many inns and beer houses in villages and along the droves as a source of liquid refreshment – but the fen dweller *would* say that. It is a wonderful place to sit for a while and daydream, with the church, the Old Hall, dated 1620, and a new medical centre at the foot of the spring, all close by. It was the epitome of a small country fen-edge village, mothers with small children feeding the ducks and the church clock chiming, somewhere to sit and escape the humdrum of modern life. Still curious, I walked to The Fortescue Arms on the main street, passing a small but no doubt excellent little butcher's shop on the way. The Fortescue Arms takes its name from the Fortescue family who were lords of the manor with a large estate around the village.

Car Dyke in Sempringham Fen

The Crown Estate today is around 14,000 acres, 60% being fen and fen-edge, the remainder being high country, and farms mostly 500 acres and upwards. On my travels I will be passing Crown Estate land stretching from Pointon to Swaton; Billingborough Common was enclosed in 1770.

Crops in 1922 were wheat, oats, barley, beans and potatoes. Today the cropping is mainly combinable crops, being typical of the area. The fen-edge from Bourne to Billingborough in the past was well known for the growing of early potatoes. Light free-draining soil, and water for irrigation, were ideal for potatoes, enabling the farmers to get onto the land in early spring and pick them even in wet conditions. One local farmer also told me that this fen-edge favoured an ecosystem ideal for growing this early crop of potatoes. I cannot say I have seen many such crops growing here in the past two decades.

CHURCH OF ST ANDREW

The church stands in the centre of the village, built of stone, of mixed styles, but mainly 14th century and Perpendicular.

The square tower has pinnacles linked by flying buttresses to a tall spire 150 feet high on the west end of the north aisle. There are two clock faces on the tower, facing west and east. The clerestories along the nave are stone mullion windows allowing ample light to illuminate the nave, which has north and south aisles, and a chancel. Inside the church one can appreciate the exceptional stained-glass windows, some with fragments of medieval glass. The nave ceiling is wood of tie-beam construction, while the chancel ceiling is also wood but of arch-braced construction.

The wooden bench-style pews are worth sitting in to admire this lovely church, time to reflect on its history and the people who have worshipped in it for many generations. Look at the lectern and pulpit and maybe imagine what words have been spoken from them in the past.

The church is well lit by the clerestories and aisle windows, with four great arches along the nave, and a porch on the south aisle. Splendid stone pillars are made up of four round columns which together make one pillar, with circular bases supporting the arches.

The stone font with a wooden cover topped with a carved wooden angel and inscription is something not to miss. The inscription reads 'To the glory of God and in loving memory of Ralph M Credland RAF VR who gave his life that others might live. January 1942. Presented by his parents R.I.P.'.

There are many interesting features in the church that must not be missed; I cannot describe them all, but I will mention a plaque in the church to Mary Gould 1829 who bequeathed monies to the poor and for the education of one or more poor children in this parish. Frank Gould was our neighbouring farmer down Sempringham Fen, whose son still farms there. I have fond memories of

Frank, who was a very kind man, and I am sure Mary must have been one of his ancestors. Leaving the church I did notice the devil's door on the north aisle.

On leaving the village I noticed an old stone house opposite the Old Hall which had been recently refurbished to a very high standard. It adds charm to the village, is pleasing to see, and hopefully provides a pleasant home for someone.

Above: *The Fortescue Arms, Billingborough*

Left: *The Spring Wells, Billingborough*

INTO THE UPLANDS

FOLKINGHAM

Having been down the fen at Dowsby I felt the impulse to go upcountry to Folkingham village. Approaching the village, my first introduction to it was the House of Correction on the right, site of a castle and prison. There are no remains of the castle or the original prison, built in 1808, only the entrance as you see it today, which was built in 1878. It was designed by Bryan Browning, a Lincolnshire architect who was also responsible for the Sessions House at Bourne, a Grade II listed building. The House of Correction is open for accommodation through The Landmark Trust, should anyone wish to stay there (www.landmarktrust.org.uk/houseofcorrection-8655).

The approach from the bottom of the village towards The Greyhound at the top is, I think, one of the finest approaches into a village as you will find in England. It is a nice village to stroll around, which I did. The Greyhound brings back memories of the Belvoir Hunt and a time when the village was full of horses, and followers of all ages who came just to watch this very old English tradition in a village that could have been built for such pageantry to be held in it. I see Quaintways is still a café serving afternoon teas, where my parents would take us for tea, sandwiches and scones, and I took my children there in the 1960s. What was tempting is the Chocolate House near Quaintways adding a touch of flavour to the village.

I have often thought the village has a Flemish look about it by the architecture of some of the houses and shops. Several of the houses in the village and some of the farmhouses in the neighbourhood have mansard roofs. The roof has its angle divided to slope more steeply in the lower part than in the upper part, increasing the area in the attic or roof. This style of roof is named after François Mansard, a 17th-century architect, who must have influenced a local architect or builder.

The House of Correction, Folkingham

I have some sale particulars dated 1920 when the Folkingham Estate was sold by auction. There were 9 farms consisting of 2,120 acres, shops and many cottages in the village. The Greyhound hotel, two licensed inns, allotments and smallholdings – almost the entire village – was sold. Also for sale was the Lordship of the Manor of Folkingham. British agriculture from the 1870s until the First World War had suffered its worst depression in its history. The war helped agricultural incomes, and farming flourished after the war until the late 1920s. Many landlords thought the depression would come again, with goods flooding in again from the Americas and the British colonies around the world. Land prices increased on the back of farm incomes and so many landowners chose to sell their estates. This was not unique to Lincolnshire; the total land sales were the largest they had ever been in history. Another reason for this great exodus of land holdings

Folkingham village

A terrace of houses with a mansard roof, Folkingham

by estate owners was the fear that Communism, after the Russian Revolution in 1917, would spread across Europe, and maybe to the UK. I was not disappointed with my visit to Folkingham, but rather nostalgic. It was just as I remember it: a quintessential English village that has not lost its charm or character.

Church of St andrew

After walking up the village towards The Greyhound I went to the church, close by. It has many styles of architecture – Perpendicular, Early Decorated and Late Transitional, with some remains of Norman work. The tower is of Perpendicular style in four stages embattled with eight pinnacles, the largest being on the four corners. The tower has a clock and contains five bells. The nave has north and south aisles, while the chancel is on the east end of the nave with vestry and clerestories, which have three windows on each side allowing ample light into the church. The devil's door is one of the finest I have seen so far, made of oak with wrought-iron hinges encased in a Norman arch surround with an ornate tympanum. The porch into the church is well worth lingering over. It has a large parvis above it and a pair of wonderfully ornate carved doors of oak. They may look relatively new, but that does not detract from the fine craftsmanship in making them.

The nave has three arches down each side, with an ancient 15th-century rood screen of dark oak, richly carved, and an organ chamber. The south porch is of particular interest with a parvis above it, and a Transitional door arch with new doors, which are of superb workmanship. Perpendicular pews with bench ends line the nave; also of interest are the stocks from the village and an antique bier. There is a fine decorated sedilia, with three seats for the clergy.

The nave ceiling is wooden arch-braced, old but I am unsure of its age. The font is most unusual being stone, resembling a fluted urn with a wooden cover topped with a crucifix.

Unlike many neighbouring villages, the population of Folkingham has not increased much. In 1911 it was 479 and today under 800.

STOW GREEN

On my way back towards Billingborough, at the first crossroads I turned right onto the Roman road of Mareham Lane up to Stow Green Hill.

My father had told me about the famous horse fair at Stow Green when I was young, at a time when we still had horses working on the farm. I had passed it several times in the past but never put my feet on the green, always rushing to or from somewhere.

In 1268 the Prior of Sempringham was granted permission to hold a fair annually on the green, from 23 to 25 June. It was originally a carnival and a fair for agricultural goods, much of them coming from Sempringham Abbey itself. The abbey farms were great wool producers, which attracted wool merchants from far and wide to the fair. Over time the activities of the fair changed from a country fair and carnival to a horse fair frequented by horse dealers, breeders, gypsies and, it is said, many undesirable vagabonds, until its closure in 1915.

Only the green remains where the fair was held, but it is good occasionally just to stand on a certain spot and dream of the sound of horses' hoofs, the animals being trotted up by their owners, the bartering and the handshake to clinch a deal, followed by the jingle of coins changing hands! Some of that would have been 'luck money', which the purchaser would ask the vendor for, to give him luck on his new purchase. Luck money was still common in the livestock trade until just a few decades ago.

While reading the information board at the green it made me think back to the Princess Gwenllian while she was at Sempringham Priory. She would have been 14 when the first fair took place and she may have attended many of the fairs – who knows? … but it is a thought.

Stow is mentioned in the Domesday Book and I was told that the Church of St Mary stood here where burial remains were found dating back to the 11th and 12th centuries. There are no visible remains left on the green.

It's a peaceful spot, quite scenic with lots of room; hard to imagine the hustle and bustle that went on here centuries ago, but all I heard was the wind through the trees, a soothing sound for the mind.

HORBLING

I drove back to the fen-edge and down to Horbling, a large, well-built village with its church and manor house dictating its character.

The Plough inn is on the opposite side of the road to the church and still in regular use. One can easily drive in and out of the village without realising you are through it; it must be a tranquil and serene place to live.

The Ouse Mere Lode passes under the road between Billingborough and Horbling, still running. Where the mere was I do not know but I suppose it must have been down in the fen itself.

CHURCH OF ST ANDREW

The church displays many periods of architecture, giving it an added charm. It is reputed to have been built by the monks of Sempringham Abbey. I was in luck when I stopped off at the church, as it was open and welcoming.

The font in the Church of St Andrew, Horbling

The church is of cruciform design, the chancel, nave and transepts forming the crossing at the base of the tower. The tower has battlements topped by pinnacles on four corners. The south porch was added in 1854, as were the pews, along with other renovations by the benefactor Benjamin Smith, a local dignitary. The nave has large mullion clerestories along the north and south aisles, with the chancel at the east end of the tower.

Inside, my eye immediately caught sight of the chancel arch, which is in the shape of a horseshoe, as well as the fine Decorated stone font with a wooden cover, 14th century.

At the west end of the nave is an exquisite stained-glass window said to date back to the 15th century. Along the nave on both sides there are four perpendicular arches supported on hexagonal pillars. The nave ceilings are always fascinating, this one being a wooden tie-beam design which must be a great age. There is a devil's door in the north aisle.

After leaving the village I went down Horbling Fen to see if there were still signs of the Car Dyke, which I did find. We know the line of the dyke, so identifying its course in certain parts is possible, but here it was only a minnow of its former glory; in fact it could be mistaken for a small fen dyke. I carried on down the fen road to the pumping station on the Forty Foot Drain to find 'space' and take a moment to ponder.

Leaving Horbling I crossed the A52 at Bridge End, once a causeway out of the fen from Donnington to Bridge End, known as a Salters Way. This route would have joined up to the Roman road of Mareham Lane near Folkingham, and crossed the Car Dyke at or near Bridge End.

There were many Romano-British salterns around the area at Bicker and Surfleet, the remains of which can still be seen today. The sites are noticeable by large mounds of silt, some as large as small hillocks, which is the silt residue of the salt-making method.

REFLECTIONS

I had travelled around 30 miles from my first sighting of the Car Dyke at Eye, to Bridge End. Considering its age and knowing that over time it would be lost in parts due to urbanisation and drainage of the fens, I had kept an open mind as to what my findings would be. I was sure on the way here that I would find significant parts of Car Dyke similar to what I had found at Eye. By Bridge End, however, I had become disillusioned, after finding so little of this ancient monument left, and what I did find resembled nothing like my first sighting. Did our ancestors not realise its historical importance and preserve some stretches of it for future generations to see?

Many things have been saved or listed as ancient monuments, of far less importance than this piece of our history. It has taken us many centuries to realise what a national treasure we have, exemplified now by the Bowstring Bridge straddling it. Much of our fenland history has been sidelined in the past – not as appealing to the eye as the uplands maybe, to some.

I must not be too pessimistic; I still have another 20 odd miles of Car Dyke to explore and many miles of fen-edge. What has impressed me are the churches I have seen on my journey, a pilgrimage in itself. One can travel the fen-edge practically never having a church out of your sight, as if they were beacons to guide the fen people to them. They are a holy divide between fen and upland, with churches close by in the west but the fenland churches lying many miles to the east. The early fen churches were built on higher ground to protect them from inundations by the sea and water from the uplands. After the drainage schemes and enclosures, fen settlements grew up and churches were built on safe ground, which had previously flooded.

THE FEN EDGE

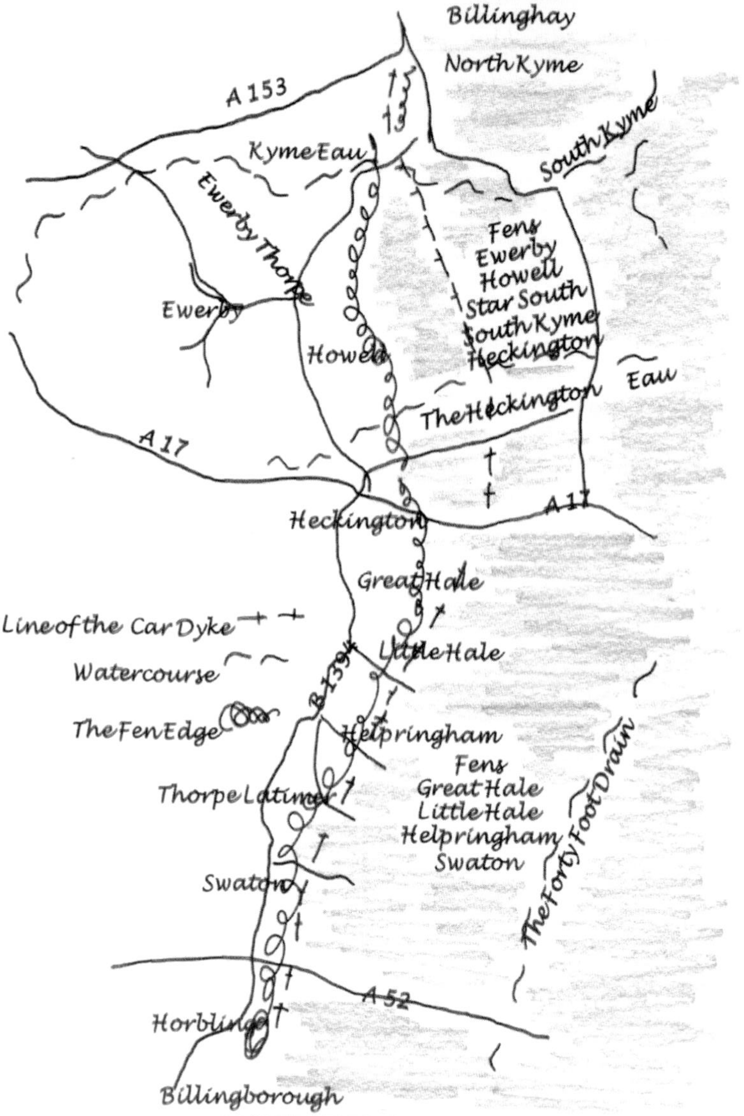

Billinghay

North Kyme

A 153

Kyme Eau

South Kyme

Ewerby Thorpe

Fens
Ewerby
Howell
Star South
South Kyme
Heckington

Ewerby

Howell

The Heckington Eau

A 17

A 17

Heckington

Great Hale

Line of the Car Dyke

Little Hale

Watercourse

B 1394

The Fen Edge

Helpringham

Fens
Great Hale
Little Hale
Helpringham
Swaton

Thorpe Latimer

The Forty Foot Drain

Swaton

A 52

Horbling

Billingborough

The Fen Edge
Billingborough
To Billinghay

SWATON TO LINCOLN

SWATON

Swaton was at one time a farming village, with the Crown Estate still owning most of the land surrounding it. Most residents in the village today are not employed on the farms; the only reminder that it was once a farming village are the remaining farmsteads scattered in and around the village itself. Having been the property of several estate owners over the centuries has left its mark, evident by the well-maintained farmsteads and substantial farmhouses. The Swaton Eau, bringing 'live water' destined for the fen from higher ground, adds a touch of charm as it trickles through the village.

I drove down Parsons Drove in the village past a fine imposing red-brick and stone house, which presumably was the former rectory, a reminder of the importance that the local incumbent held in the community in the past. Not that the clergy of today are not looked up to with reverence and standing in the community, but most of their homes would not compare to the rectories of the past.

The former Rectory, Swaton

Car Dyke in Swaton Fen, showing where it has been in-filled

I noticed on my OS map that further down Parsons Drove was Car Dyke Farm, so I knew I was somewhere near the line of the Car Dyke itself. Some way before the farm I came across it. It was well defined on the northern side of the road but there was no sign of it going south. It was obviously not needed as a water carrier and so had been filled in to enlarge the fields on either side of its original course.

Later, when I was at home, I looked on Google Earth to try to follow the filled-in part of the Dyke. It was easy to trace the line as crop marks to where it crossed the A52, where it was still a watercourse across Horbling Fen.

White's Lincolnshire Directories 1882 and *1842* mention 'most of the soil belonging to Henry James Lee-Warner of Walsingham'. The Lee-Warners were a prominent landowning and religious Norfolk family going back several generations. Their estate must have changed hands after 1882 since *Kelly's Directory of Lincolnshire 1922* mentions much of the soils belonging to the Crown Estate. This estate was added to their Billingborough estate which was purchased in 1855. In 1882 the parish of Swaton had 3,150 acres of land to its name, of which 940 acres were in Swaton Fen, which had been enclosed in 1805.

CHURCH OF ST MICHAEL

On entering the village the site of this imposing building gives the village an air of substance. White mentions its origin being 13th century, from Henry III to Edward III period. It is a large, imposing cruciform building, the tower being between the nave and the chancel. The tower has pinnacles, decorated with crockets and four stone gargoyles on each corner of the embattled tower. The nave has north and south aisles, and battlements along the roof line, with a porch on the south aisle.

The tower has transepts on the north and south sides forming a crossing. On the west end of the church there are three windows, one in each aisle and a very large one in the nave, filling almost the entire end of the nave itself. I am sure when the sun is setting light will stream through those windows and make a matins service almost like being in heaven. I would like to have seen inside the church, especially since it was so impressive outside, but it was locked.

On the south transept is a memorial stone in memory of five children who died under the age of seven years. They were the children of Michael and Bridget Moore who all died between 1828 and 1839.

No doubt the Lee-Warners' religious dedication had its influence in this fine church and elegant former rectory.

THORPE LATIMER

Leaving Swaton I soon arrived at Thorpe Latimer which was the seat of the Latimer family, mentioned in the 12th century, Thorpe being a secondary settlement of Helpringham. Today it is hardly a settlement but rather a farmstead and the occasional cottage. Adjoining the farm is an ancient meadow with some very old trees and the remains of a moat which must once have encircled a manorial building or buildings.

I knew the Watts, whose family lived and farmed here in the past, so I drove into the farmyard, welcomed by the sight of Lincoln Red cattle in the cattle yard. Some of the old farm buildings had been converted into a horse livery yard, with several horses to show for it along with keen youngsters handling them – it was so pleasing to see the farmyard busy.

One building had been turned into a café, so I went in to enquire about the Watts family. What hit me as I entered was the smell of newly baked bread and scones as they came out of the oven, handled by Nathan, who runs the Shrub and Grub Café and artisan bakery along with Abi Eaves. We chatted about the Watts family whom he confirmed were Will and Ann Watts, still farming there and the cattle were theirs. A friendly chap Nathan, who chatted more, about where he was from and what made him start the café and bakery out in the country. He came from Birmingham, studied in Lincoln and liked 'the fen area and catering', so that was it. Well no it wasn't, I had to buy some scones straight from the oven which I took home and enjoyed enormously – in fact I had one for breakfast the next day as well. I was pleased I did call in and will again if I'm passing. I wish them good luck in their business and am sure local people will support them, as well as travellers like myself.

Henry III granted the right to hold a market and a fair there – who knows, maybe one day we will see it held again.

HELPRINGHAM

Approaching Helpringham the road rises out of the fen to cross a railway line. So what is so unusual about that, one might ask? Only that one rarely has the good fortune in the fens of having an aerial view of the surrounding landscape while waiting for the gates to open to allow one through.

Lord Willoughby de Brooke was once lord of the manor of Helpringham and a landowner here. *White's 1882* also mentions him as being heir-general to the Latimers, taking the title Baron Latimer.

CHURCH OF ST ANDREW

Entering the village I was impressed by the tall, elegant tower and spire of the church, almost standing in the middle of the road. The tower on the west end of the nave has four embattled pinnacles with flying buttresses dressed with crockets reaching up into the fenland sky, as if trying to grasp a passing cloud. Entrance

to the church is via the porch, which is on the south aisle. Two clocks adorn the tower on the east and west sides.

At the base of the tower inside the church there are four tall arches leading to the north and south aisles and the nave, and one to the bell-ringers' quarters where there are five bells. It gave me a feeling of serenity standing beneath them and looking up. The nave is well lit by clerestories, with a tie-beam wooden ceiling with arched brace supporting four rows of wooden panels in the roof, which looked magnificent in the afternoon sunlight.

Four Perpendicular round stone arches divide the nave from the aisles, all being identical. The chancel is divided from the nave by a decorative chancel screen and an altar screen, in between which are the choir stalls and the organ. A sedilia features near the altar. There were several interesting features which caught my eye in this church: an ancient bier, the bench pews with elegant bench-ends with finials, the pulpit made of wood on a stone base, and a fine brass lectern. The stone font, complete with an elegant cover, is described in *English Church Furniture* as being of Norman origin. I have visited many fine churches on my wanderings which I could not get access to, so I don't know what hidden treasures I might have seen inside. I was lucky with this one being open, and could happily have stayed longer in this church. It was well kept, and welcoming to visit, thanks to its dedicated wardens and parishioners.

The church is close to the village green on which a war memorial stands dedicated to the villagers who died in the Second World War. Near the memorial is The Brass Windmill inn, and open for business, which is always good to see. An old chapel stands near the green, as does a very old stone house, which is boarded up and in need of restoration. Back in the 1960s many fen areas were becoming depopulated and properties were demolished or left to become run down. The past 20 years have seen a reverse with people wishing to retire to or live in rural areas and fen villages. With improved transport facilities and the internet, people can work from home or just live in the countryside. This has brought life into many rural areas and a restoration of rundown properties. I am sure the old stone house I had just seen will be brought back to its former glory and enhance the village. The village green adds to the charm of the village. *White's 1882* mentions an ancient stone cross with steps and pedestal, which is still there without the cross (www.helpringham.org.uk).

The book on the Car Dyke by the Heritage Trust of Lincolnshire (HTL) notes that there was an SSSI section of the Car Dyke at Helpringham Fen, so I left the village and drove down the fen road. After about a mile the road starts to veer towards the railway line, where the Car Dyke is visible alongside some tall haw-thorn bushes at the edge of an old meadow. Many Iron Age and Romano-British artefacts have been found here, signifying the importance of the Car Dyke. It is on private land here so access is not allowed to the site, which the HTL deems probably the best-preserved section anywhere along the entire route of the Car Dyke. I was extremely lucky that day in meeting the farmer, Nev Barnes, who owns the field and allowed me to walk across the site. Maybe being a farmer myself helped me get along with Nev whose family has farmed here for several generations and who has a great passion for the countryside.

With so many finds of various artefacts from human activities, especially from the Romano-British era, it seems ever more likely that the Car Dyke was used mainly for transport rather than as a catchwater. Salterns are also known to have been in this area.

As I left the village travelling towards Little Hale I crossed a fine bridge over the Helpringham Eau. It is of red brick construction with triple arches and I would say built in the 19th century, Grade II listed. Looking at the size of the arches it was built to cope with a large flow of water in the Eau, which brings water from the heathland around Sleaford and west around Oasby some 20 miles away.

The North and South Becks merge into the Helpringham Eau five miles to the west of Helpringham at Burton Cliff. It then runs between Little Hale Fen and Helpringham Fen, the water being pumped into the South Forty Foot Drain.

Helpringham village green

The Car Dyke in Helpringham Fen

The Red Bridge (Grade II listed) over the Helpringham Eau

I have to mention these water carriers into the fen, and cannot forget the phrase from the past, 'bringing live water into the fen', meaning the highland waters. The Car Dyke would have gathered water from such becks, either as a catchwater drain, or for navigation, whichever purpose it was designed for.

GREAT HALE

The road winds its way through Little Hale and on to Great Hale where the church tower caught my eye, so I stopped to take a closer look. This village was once called 'Hale Magna'.

CHURCH OF ST JOHN THE BAPTIST

The church has a lofty square Norman tower topped with a parapet adorned with eight pinnacles, with a clock on the west front of the tower. The tower and much of the church is built of small sandstones, resembling those used in stone walls around fields (I am sure there must be a term for such masonry work). The nave has north and south aisles with the porch on the south aisle. Entrance to the porch is through a plain blunt-shaped arch; above that is a figure of Christ set in a niche. *Rawnsley 1926* mentions that the chancel was pulled down around the 17th century, but the end arch of the nave can still be seen on the outside east end of the church. This end of the church is impressive with its three mullion windows, the centre nave window being stained glass. I would liked to have seen inside the church since Rawnsley also mentions several interesting subjects and writes 'to antiquarians I consider that this is one of the most interesting of Lincolnshire churches'. However, I do understand the reasons for locking the churches when services are not taking place; it is sign of the times we live in.

The east end of the Church of St John the Baptist, Great Hale

I suppose I could have enquired for the key holder but I did not, so maybe it was partly my own fault for not entering the church. The church is plain erect and stands with a proud air of itself, giving the impression it will serve many generations to come, if people choose to support it.

There is an attractive old stone house at the side of the church with a pantile roof and lattice windows. Otherwise most of the houses are built of brick and relatively modern, with only a smattering of stone houses around the village. Much of the parish extends into Great Hale Fen, which was enclosed in 1700.

HECKINGTON

Only a short distance from Great Hale, on the B1394, I entered the village of Heckington and was greeted by the sight of a large windmill, the only eight-sail windmill in the UK. It was restored some years ago to working order and one cannot miss it as you drive into the village, standing loftily near the railway level crossing.

Heckington Show is held annually on the last weekend in July. The first one was held in 1864 and it is claimed to be the largest village show in England. I did go to it many years ago and maybe ought to go again to help keep old traditions alive (www.heckingtonshow.org.uk).

I parked in the centre of the village on the green near the war memorial cross. It was a sunny day and time to stretch my legs and have a wander. Around the green is a tearoom and wine bar opposite The Nag's Head inn. At the opposite end of the green are two attractive almshouses. Their red-brick construction with lattice windows painted white glittered in the sun, giving the green an air of serenity and a step back in time. They were donated in 1886 by Henry Godson, whose name I recalled in *White's 1882*. White mentioned the church tower as 'having a good clock and eight bells, two being added in 1881 through the liberality of E Godson Esq', the Godsons being a local landowning family. I don't know if there are Godsons still in the locality but if not their name is marked in time in Heckington. How nice to see such people remembered for their generosity to others; they took nothing out of this world but left something to the village to admire. Towering above the roofs of the almshouses was the village church spire, beckoning me to make a visit, as well as drawing me away from the inviting Nag's Head inn.

Walking down Church Street I could not help but notice the Methodist chapel, a fine brick building with twin doors set in a stone surround, above which is a beautiful stone mullion window. It was built in 1840, three years after Queen Victoria came to the throne, an era of great prosperity when many fine Methodist chapels were built, especially in the fens. Also in the street was a café and coffee house and a small village store near the church, all adding an insight into village life there. I must add that the village store had a for sale sign on its wall. I hope someone buys it and carries on the shop, for we are losing too many such amenities in our competitive world.

Heckington mill, which has eight sails

The Godson almshouses in Heckington

I saw a spire reach up into the sky
Up to the clouds and vapour trails,
Reaching up to touch God's hand
From off the fen, this holy land.

CHURCH OF ST ANDREW

White's 1882 describes this church as 'a large and handsome structure', while Rawnsley comments that it is 'one of the wonders of Lincolnshire'. Approaching it along Church Lane, I have to agree with both. It stands as if it has erupted from this tiny island in the fens, reaching up to claim a part of the fenland sky. The Church of St Andrew is a Grade I listed building, rebuilt in the reign of Henry III. Bardney Abbey had a chancery here in the 13th century and it is due to their goodwill that such a fine church was built.

The tower on the west end of the nave has a tall spire with pinnacles, a clock and eight bells in the lofty belfry. The nave is tall and imposing with clerestories with fine mullion windows on both sides. There is a north aisle and south aisle with a porch. The porch is wonderfully ornate, and must be seen. The church from the outside has many interesting features: gargoyles, balustrades, figures of animals, a priest's door, ornate pinnacles and niches, all of which captured my interest.

The chancel has a vestry on the north side with an exceptional stained-glass window at the east end. I was amazed by the splendour of this parish church and was even more astonished when I went inside. Wooden pews line the nave leading up to the chancel, with ornate choir stalls in front of the altar, which has a stone blind arcade behind it. The large stained-glass window at the east end of the chancel illuminates the church. A hexagonal stone font is enriched with highly decorated niches.

Another interesting feature is the elegant timber gallery which crosses the west end of the nave above the tower arch. I am sure my description of this fine church does not do it justice.

Heckington, the Church of St Andrew, north aisle

I also visited the Heritage Trust of Lincolnshire, at The Old School, Cameron Street. They have carried out extensive archaeological work over many years and published their works, which I have used in the past. Their reports can be purchased at their office in the Old School.

REFLECTIONS

Walking back from the church to my car I had time to reflect on my journey along the fen-edge. Since leaving Eye I had travelled, with diversions, 40–50 miles along my intended route. My intentions had been to follow the Car Dyke. I had found few traces of it, some of which could be mistaken for small fen dykes, but its route is still well defined. What I had found on the way was 21 churches, from grand structures to a 'tin tabernacle' and small parish churches, some ancient, some not so ancient. They were fen-edge churches, having an historical connection with the fen and the uplands, neither laying claim to either, but shared by both. Not all the churches were open for me to see inside, but I prized the exteriors of all of them, reading names on the gravestones, seeing plaques relating to old families and benefactors, all of whom had worshipped in these churches. Some of the family names still exist in the parishes, some do not, but many are remembered for their dedication to their individual churches. I saw plaques commemorating those who had died for their country, at home and in foreign parts. Many babies would have been held in the arms of the local priest at the beautiful fonts I had seen on my journey, and many would have been married and buried in the same churches. Generations have passed through the porches I have passed through. I felt I was privileged to have entered their holy grounds. My journey was changing from a fact-finding tour of the Car Dyke to a holy pilgrimage along the fen-edge – sacred ground indeed.

Planning my wanderings north from Heckington along the fen-edge leaves me in a quandary of which route to take to stay on the fen-edge. My map tells me to stay on the OS 5 metre contour up to Howell and Ewerby but my desire to follow the Car Dyke which the Romans took tells me differently.

The line of the Car Dyke from Helpringham heading north moves east away from the fen-edge and below the OS 5 metre contour line. It goes deeper into the fen itself, almost as if it had lost its way. By the time I got to Heckington it was well off the fen and crossing Star Fen and Howell Fen. It could have returned to the fen on the west and gone up the lower ground towards Metheringham through the low ground to Nocton Woods, and joined its present line.

The Romans, however, did not take this route, but instead made a cut to Billinghay via South Kyme and North Kyme. This may have been to intersect the Old Slea River and the Billinghay Skirth, if they existed then as water carriers. If that was the case, it would have linked the Car Dyke to the River Witham and the sea, or even the port of Wainfleet, which we know the Romans used. Navigable access to Sleaford would have also been connected to the Roman roads of Mareham Lane and Ermine Street. These are only my assumptions for which

I have no facts. After Billinghay it joins the fen-edge up past Walcot, Martin and Blankney Wood, hugging the edge of the cliff edge to Lincoln.

Curious to see why the Romans should have gone deeper into the fen east of Heckington, I decided to go and look for any visible signs of the Car Dyke.

I drove east on the road from the village which meets the B1395 and knew if there were any remains of it they might be visible from this road. Sure enough after about a mile down the road I saw a drain, the Car Dyke, taking water up to the Heckington Eau, which I could see embanked in the distance. It was heading to the west of South Kyme tower which is on the 5 metre contour line running from Billinghay. What I could have done was take the footpath from Heckington which runs east past the sewage works along the Heckington Eau and seen where they met.

This far out from the fen-edge to the west makes me think even more that it was not a catchwater drain, rather a navigation drain, since catchwater drains mostly run close to the fen-edge.

Wishing to stay as close to the fen-edge as possible and with no plan in mind I decided to go across to Howell.

Line of the Car Dyke east of Heckington along Star Fen, its furthest point away from the fen-edge

HOWELL

The small church greets you as you enter the village, with the manor house close by, making a tranquil scene. There are some substantial stone houses in the village although the manor house is built of brick. I went down the road to Howell Fen, where soils quickly change from gravel content to fen. The land is well farmed and it was there I enjoyed the view from down in the fen across to Kyme Tower in the distance, and to the towering spires of Ewerby and Heckington.

On the way back to the village I called in to Manor Farm where I met Mark Sarderson who is the seventh generation to farm that land. Mark said that there was once a castle in the village and when it was demolished the stone was used to build some of the houses, hence the several stone houses.

CHURCH OF ST OSWALD

The church is an ancient structure consisting of nave and chancel with an aisle on the north side of the nave with clerestories. The porch is Norman and stands on the south side of the nave. There is no tower, rather a substantial structure forming a bellcote on the west end of the nave with space for two bells, although it has only the one. Mark told me that the other bell was sold to raise money for restoration, which may have been in 1870 when major restoration work was carried out. The church was locked but I was told it only seats around 70 people. To the traveller who is lucky enough to find the church open, Cox and Harvey's *English Church Furniture* mentions a heraldic font from the Perpendicular period, one of only three in Lincolnshire.

From Howell I headed north to Ewerby Thorpe, and then into Ewerby Fen where Kyme Tower in the distance again caught my attention, and my curiosity. The crops were cereals, sugar beet and oilseed rape, along with maize on the medium to heavy soils. The area appeared very well farmed, with several new hedges planted along the roads. Further into the fen I could see an embankment running eastwards towards South Kyme. As a fenman I realised it had to be a river or drain, being higher than the surrounding land, as many upland watercourses cross the fens. It was the River Slea, which I followed to Ferry Farm.

Here the Slea meets the Car Dyke and joins it for a short distance before flowing into the Kyme Eau. The Eau then journeys across low fenland to Chapel Hill on the east bank of the River Witham.

I stopped and stood on the bridge at Ferry Farm, a pretty and secluded spot, to watch the water flowing beneath the bridge.

SOUTH KYME

The village lies on the banks of the Kyme Eau, which is fed by the River Slea. The Slea gathers it water from around the Roman village of Ancaster then flows through Sleaford and on to South Kyme where it meets the Car Dyke.

Around the 13th century the Slea was linked by the Kyme Eau to cross South Kyme Fen to Chapel Hill on the River Witham below Tattershall, passing through seven locks on its way. The railways brought about its demise, and many other navigable waterways in the 19th century suffered the same fate. The Sleaford Navigation Trust are working to restore the whole section from Sleaford to Chapel Hill; I wish them good luck in their endeavours.

The manor and castle were the seat of the Kyme family dating back to the 13th century, the tower being the only remains of the castle, standing erect on a green field surrounded by the remains of a moat. The castle was demolished between 1720 and 1725, the stone being used to build farmhouses in the vicinity, several of which remain today.

South Kyme Tower

An idyllic spot to stroll around is the tower, which dominates the green over-looked by the old manor house. The manor house stands in an imposing position, the front part being of stone; what looks like a later addition enlarging the house is brick. There were some black cattle grazing in a paddock below the manor as I walked around the green, and the church reflected a glint of sun, the tower stating its presence. The scene somehow stirred my love of rural England. I was not in the fen or the uplands but in another part of Lincolnshire, one I lived so close to but did not know – the fen-edge. I stood on the bridge over the Eau and watched the water passing slowly underneath my feet, coming from somewhere and going somewhere.

It could have been a scene from the castle's halcyon days … but it was not, it was the present, which brought to mind a quotation by Alice Morse Earle, an American poet: 'Yesterday is history, tomorrow is a mystery, and today is a gift and that is why it is called the present' – poignant words, especially in that setting.

I was brought back to the present when a large tractor with a plough started ploughing a recently lifted sugar beet field in preparation for another cycle in the farming calendar. I drove out of the village, passing the old school built in 1843 which is now a private residence with the schoolhouse alongside. It was nice to see The Hume inn looking shipshape and inviting – lucky residents to still have a local inn. The Kyme Eau flowing through the village adds a touch of nostalgia, and maybe the efforts to open the watercourse for navigation will bring some history to life again. This ridge of higher ground on which South Kyme stands reaches out into the fen from Martin in the north down to Billinghay, following the OS 10 and 5 metre contour lines.

CHURCH OF ST MARY AND ALL SAINTS

The church is a tall building without a traditional tower or spire. The great porch has a fine entrance arch under a niche with a worn sculpture of the Coronation of the Virgin. The church has fragments of stone in the north wall with knotwork and other ornaments certainly carved by Saxons. A wall monument supported by figures of Time and Death is in memory of a parish clerk's son, Marmaduke Dickinson. The church was locked when I made my visit – disappointing but understandable in modern times. I am sure if I had really wished to go inside more of the locked churches on my journey, it could have been arranged. I am, though, a person who likes to be free of time and tide, to wander as and when I please, and take the consequences. The church is one of the Car Dyke Group of Parishes, along with Martin, North Kyme, Timberland, Walcott and Billinghay.

Contact can be made via wwwlincoln.ourchurchweb.org.uk if needed.

It was time to move on, although I was sad to leave so tranquil a spot as South Kyme. I headed north, still on the high ridge to North Kyme, where the land sweeps down and blends into the fen on both sides of the road, Kyme Fen on the right, Digby Fen on my left – 'double fen'. There were no visible signs of the Car Dyke along the way.

The line of the Car Dyke on the A153 between North Kyme and Billinghay

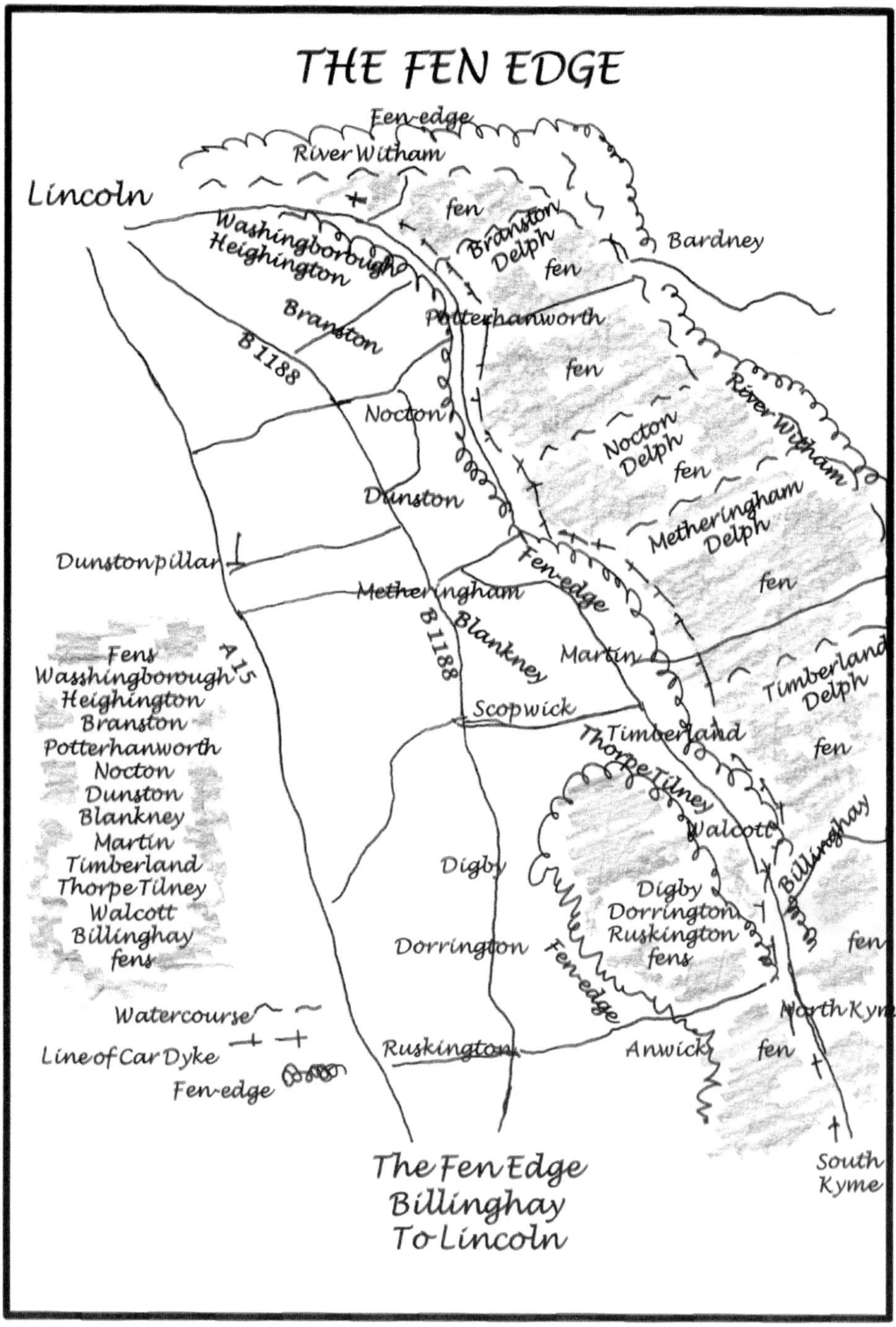

THE FEN EDGE

Fen-edge

River Witham

Lincoln

Fen-edge

Bardney

Washingborough
Heighington

fen

Branston
Delph

fen

Branston

B 1188

Potterhanworth

River Witham

fen

Nocton

Nocton
Delph

fen

Dunston

Metheringham
Delph

Dunstonpillar

Metheringham

Fen-edge

fen

B 1188

Blankney

Martin

Timberland
Delph

Fens
Wasshingborough
Heighington
Branston
Potterhanworth
Nocton
Dunston
Blankney
Martin
Timberland
ThorpeTilney
Walcott
Billinghay
fens

A 15

Scopwick

Timberland

fen

Thorpe Tilney

Digby

Walcott

Billinghay

Digby
Dorrington
Ruskington
fens

fen

Dorrington

Fenedge

Watercourse

North Kyme

Line of Car Dyke

Ruskington

Anwick

fen

Fen-edge

South
Kyme

The Fen Edge
Billinghay
To Lincoln

NORTH KYME

North Kyme has a church, St Luke's, also part of the Car Dyke Group of Parishes, as well as The Plough inn and, to complete the rural scene, Burdens Agricultural Machinery Dealers – yes, it is farming country.

REFLECTIONS

Having crossed many watercourses on the journey, it was a good time to reflect on the flows of water coming into the fens from the west, and the catchment areas they will pass through before entering the Wash.

On my journey along the fen-edge between Peakirk and North Kyme, there are broadly speaking two catchment areas. Between Peakirk and Bourne all watercourses drain into the Rivers Welland and Glen, the latter discharging into the River Welland at Surfleet Seas End. Between Bourne and North Kyme all watercourses drain into the Forty Foot Drain which itself discharges into the Haven at Boston. North of North Kyme to Lincoln, all watercourses drain into the River Witham. Bourne and North Kyme, one could say, are the dividing points for fenland waters. Being a fenman the management of water is most important to me, as it is to those living in the fens themselves. We must also not forget that practically all the fenland is below the OS 5 metre contour line, a line I have been hopping either side of since I started my journey.

Pondering at North Kyme I felt I had gone far enough, and was missing another mysterious part of the fen, so I back-tracked towards South Kyme and went back across the fen to Ewerby Thorpe and on to Ewerby village. I was now back on the line of the fen-edge I had followed from Billingborough to Heckington.

EWERBY

The village of Ewerby greets you from a distance with the sight of the church steeple towering above the village. And it was not alone: in the distance I could see more than one church steeple gleaming in the sun. My farming genes always take my eyes to the soil, not fen here but more mineral soil, supporting good crops of wheat and oilseed rape. There are several stone houses and some thatched cottages in the village. One little thatched cottage was covered in a tarpaulin waiting for restoration, thankfully being saved by some loving owner.

The church dominates the village, with some fine houses and cottages adding to its charm, especially the manor opposite the church. There is a Methodist chapel, erected in 1879 and now converted to a house.

CHURCH OF ST ANDREW

The lofty tower supports a broach spire in which I believe are ten bells. The nave and chancel share the same roofline and have fine geometrical windows. The north and south aisles have no clerestories, but I imagine the large windows on the nave and especially the one at the east end would allow sufficient light into the church. The porch is on the south aisle and somewhat unusual in that it has triangular stringcourse over the hood moulding, which is most decorative.

White's 1882 mentions some pews with carved ends from the 17th century; Rawnsley notes that there are ten bells on the tower. Sadly the church was locked so I could not enter and confirm their writings. Rawnsley also claims the tower and spire to be probably the best example of a broach spire in all England, and being 174 feet high, it certainly drew me to the village.

A large house near the church with farm buildings beside it gives it a rural feel. *White's 1882* mentions the cross in front of the church being erected by Sir Ranulph Rye in the reign of Edward I when he was granted a charter to hold a market here.

The Finch Hatton Arms, Ewerby

I read descriptions of buildings and churches by travel writers of the past but I am at times sceptical of their writings. Rawnsley himself in his preface writes, 'all writers make use of the labours of their predecessors, this is inevitable and a custom as old as time'. I have sometimes found that mistakes made by the original authors are then passed on down the line. We are fortunate today in our high-tech world to be able to research on the internet and indeed check where we have been on Google Earth. This does not mean we are infallible, though; mistakes can be and still are made of the 'facts' around us.

I passed The Finch Hatton Arms, a name which brought back recollections of the Karen Blixen book *Out of Africa* and her association with Denys Finch-Hatton. His family, the Winchilseas, owned large estates here including the Haverholme estate, until the post First World War years. Like many other estates of the great landowners, it was sold following the rise in land prices after the war, and to pay death duties for those killed in the Great War.

Haverholme Priory was once a priory of the Gilbertine order of monks and nuns whose origins were at Sempringham on the fen near Billingborough. I visited the church there on my earlier journey.

I left Ewerby, pleased to have made a detour to visit such a lovely village and surrounding countryside, confirming my belief that there are indeed many beautiful villages lining the fen-edge.

I decided to follow the fen after Ewerby to Anwick. This road takes you through the wooded area of Haverholme Priory Park. I could see it was the site of a house of some standing by the remaining estate buildings and what was once parkland. I also crossed the old River Slea and the newer River Slea. It was a pleasant journey through that estate, or what remains of it.

ANWICK

Approaching Anwick I soon found the church, my second siting of a broach spire.

CHURCH OF ST EDITH

A broach spire decorated with crockets, with louvre belfry windows on the tower and the spire itself, surmounts the tower. With so many openings, it must let everyone know in the village and surrounding fields when the bells are rung. Around the base of the spire are corbel tables highly decorated with crockets, and at each corner are also highly ornate broaches. Other small windows adorn the tower almost to its finial. The porch is on the south aisle with an Early English decorated arch at the entrance.

Rawnsley mentions Anwick having a pretty church with broach spire and a good Early English doorway. The church was not open on my visit but seeing the church as it is today, I was very impressed by the broach spire, more decorative than Ewerby and extremely well kept, a credit to the village itself.

RUSKINGTON

My next port of call was Ruskington, another village I had never set foot in before but when I arrived I felt at home. *White's 1842* mentions 'the large village on a plain with a fine stream running through it'. The village was busy with shoppers enjoying the few remaining shops and café along the main street, which is divided by the trickling clear water of the beck. The beck, which gathers its waters from up on the heath after passing through this village, joins the Sleaford Canal at Haverholme Priory.

As I wandered down the main street I felt the village had an air of tranquillity about it, a feeling of spring with the trees all in blossom lining the beck. The Shoulder of Mutton inn gleamed, with the sunlight reflected from its white walls, proudly flying the Lincolnshire flag on its staff. It's a fen-edge village, claiming its own fen to the east.

Left: *The Beck running along the main Street in Ruskington.* Right: *The Shoulder of Mutton inn, Ruskington*

CHURCH OF ALL SAINTS

The church stands at the end of the main street, perched on a bend in the road. It stands its ground, with traffic going past as it has done since the Norman period.

It consists of a broad, plain low tower with a clock on the east side visible to the village. It once had a spire on the tower, which fell down in 1620 and was not replaced (*White's 1882*).

The nave and chancel have tiled roofs, with north and south aisles. There is a devil's door on the south side of the chancel. The porch is on the south aisle with decorated tympanum leading into the nave. The church was locked so I could not enter, but with no clerestories and small windows it could be dark inside. Having got as far as the porch and seen the tympanum made up for my not being able to see inside this church. Tympanums are characteristic of the Norman and Gothic periods. This was another extremely well-maintained church. Our parish churches may not have the congregations they once had, but those that are left are dedicated to their churches' survival.

DIGBY

White's 1882 refers to Digby as 'a retired village'; what he means by this I do not know. The day I went there I could say without a doubt it was a sleepy village. From the top of the village I followed the road down past a curious small structure. Someone said it was an old baking oven, which I had my doubts about, since there was no hole in the top for a chimney. It had a small door to enter through –

for what? An entrance to a well maybe? If it was an overnight lock-up for felons, like the one I saw at Deeping St James, it would not hold many such people – or maybe there were few felons in Digby in the olden days!

Since the village was sleepy, or as White would say 'retired', and no one was about, my curiosity would have to stay unsolved. However, Rawnsley mentions a 'curious lock-up, like a covered wellhead, and hardly capable of holding more than one man at a time'.

Further on down the village there is an old market cross in the middle of the road near The Red Lion inn, still complete, whereas most of the old market crosses have had the tops broken off. The Red Lion inn, referred to in *White's 1882*, was open for business and well supported after a major refurbishment a few years ago.

The Digby Beck running through Digby village

The altar screen in the Church of St Thomas a Becket, Digby

Close to The Red Lion inn the Digby Beck bringing crystal-clear spring water from the limestone aquifer under Lincoln Heath enters the village. As it meets the main street it turns to follow the street, running parallel to it on its way to the fen, depicting a perfect tranquil village scene.

CHURCH OF ST THOMAS A BECKET

This bold upright church stands up above the road which is close by. The tower is surmounted with a spire decorated with crockets up to the golden rooster at the summit. Decorated pinnacles on each corner of the ornate embattled tower add to this sturdy Gothic structure. The nave is tall, also embattled, with large clerestories along its entire length towering above the north and south aisles, while the chancel is tall and upright. It is not a large church, but it has a noble appearance adding to the charm of the village. The interior is well lit by the clerestories reflecting the light off the white walls. Interesting features are the altar screen, the sedilia at the side of the altar, and the arches lining the nave. The wooden bench pews are worth a mention with their ornate carved ends, probably the most interesting I have seen so far on my journey. *White's 1883* mentions the church as being 'a neat Gothic fabric, which was restored and the chancel rebuilt from designs by Mr Kirk in 1881'.

My last ports of call, at Ruskington and Digby, were such picturesque villages with 'live water running into the fens', I thought I would drive on to Scopwick to see if it had similar features. The road I took from Ruskington past Dorrington Digby up to Scopwick is between the OS 20 and 30 metre contour lines, which for a fen-man is getting into the clouds. Was I wandering too far from the fen? Maybe – but as I said in my introduction, I would go wherever my curiosity took me.

I was not disappointed with the journey through Rowston up to Scopwick and even more pleased to have visited Scopwick. Scopwick Beck runs through the centre of the village, trickling gin-clear water from up on heath. It has mani-cured grass banks each side as well as a road on either side of the beck.

Two teenagers sat on the banks of the beck enjoying the afternoon sun whilst reading, a peaceful scene which made me realise what we have on our doorstep, or should I say fen-edge.

Could I call it a fen village? It is only a few miles from Digby Fen, and the villagers let live water into the fens for the fenmen to dispose of. I dare to call it fen-edge, but maybe the residents would scowl at such a suggestion. Interestingly, in *White's 1882 Directory* most of the farmers and farm bailiffs listed are in Digby Fen, denoting how the village was dependent on that fen.

REFLECTIONS

I am now starting to understand why the Romans chose not to follow this route. If they had taken this route from Heckington to Scopwick, they would have had to excavate through higher ground from Rowston up to Metheringham Barff to join the fen at Nocton. With the fen petering out just north of Digby Fen I will have to back-track to Dorrington village and across Dorrington Fen to Billing-hay to try to pick up the line of the Car Dyke (see the map on page 106).

The Dorrington Dike

Crossing Dorrington Fen, the soils quickly change from a mineral content to more organic fen, with crops also changing to include sugar beet and potatoes in the rotation. The landscape is void of hedges and trees except for the occasional newly planted ones. Two embanked drains running on either side and into the distance also convince me that I am back in the fen. They bring the water off the higher ground on the edge of the heath safely across the low-lying land to Billinghay, to be diverted eventually to the Wash.

These high-water drains, as we fen people call them, are managed by the EA, not the IDBs. Fenland watercourses have always fascinated me and always will. In order to survive, our ancestors were dedicated to water management, of both the water running down into the fens and the water that falls onto the fen itself. As I approached Billinghay the drain on my left was shown as the Dorrington Dike on my OS 1998 map, but looking at my OS first edition (1824), it was called the Skirt Dike, and after leaving Billinghay going across the fen, it is the Billinghay Skirt Drain.

I could find no definition of 'skirt', in drainage terms, but I'm fascinated by its use as a drainage channel, the only one I have found in the fens. According to *Chambers Dictionary of Etymology*, the figurative sense of a border or edge is first recorded in Middle English about 1470. It could have been named the Skirt Dike as a drain bringing water from the fen-edge between Dorrington and Digby, to another fen-edge at Billinghay – just another of my assumptions. The more modern maps name it Billinghay Skirth.

BILLINGHAY

Billinghay sits on a peninsular tip of land, stretching from Martin in the north, through Timberland and Walcott to the village itself, and is surrounded by fens.

Historically it must have been in an important position for drainage and transport. *White's 1882* says 'it is a large and improving village on the navigable Car Dyke'. It would also have been a navigable link to the River Witham via the Billinghay Skirth Drain near Tattershall, while the embanked Skirth would also have acted as a causeway. It is a fen-edge village as such but with strong fen ancestry, having The Carrs and Ring Moor on its doorsteps, along with its own Billinghay Fen.

Its parish stretches across the fen to the River Witham including Dogdyke and Walcott just north of the village. A Roman burial ground was discovered between this village and Walcott, which was not far from the Car Dyke.

Car Dyke in Billinghay village near the Carrs

There are three inns in the village: The Golden Cross, The Ship and The Coach and Horses – and to keep it agricultural, there is also Padleys feed mill. The houses are mostly brick-built. One name that caught my eye was Fitzwilliam Place, a name I knew, so my curiosity led me down to it. The family was one of the great coalmining barons in Yorkshire and one of the wealthiest in the UK, at a time when coal was king. I thought I might find a place surrounded by Georgian houses tucked behind the village, knowing their grand houses, Wentworth Woodhouse and Milton Park near Peterborough. My spirits faded, but I did find the village hall and football pitch there amongst some small houses. The family had estates here, and at Digby in the 18th century, and it was the Earl Fitzwilliam who financed the cutting of what is now the South Forty Foot Drain, once known as Earl Fitzwilliam's Drain. Earl Fitzwilliam is mentioned in *White's Directory 1882*, as patron and impropriator of the church.

CHURCH OF ST MICHAEL AND ALL ANGELS

The church of St Michael is part of the Carr Dyke Group of Parishes. It displays many periods of architecture, from the 12th through to the 19th century. It's a tall, upstanding church. The tower on the west end of the nave consists of two stages with a spire, pinnacles joined by flying buttresses on each corner, with a clock and three bells.

The spire was rebuilt in 1787. Inscribed in stone above the clock's date are the letters W K. The spire is similar to a broach spire but known as a splayfoot spire, with the broaches tapering to the top of the tower walls. The nave has clerestories, north and south aisles with a chancel on the east end. The porch is on the south aisle. As you enter the church, you are greeted by a stone font of the Perpendicular period with a plain wooden cover surmounted with a crucifix. It must have witnessed the baptism of many generations of local children, if only it could talk. The north aisle is almost double the size of the south aisle. Inside the nave the wooden ceiling has heavy beams supporting the roof, of a double tie-beam construction. The upper tie beams have wooden carved bosses, which look like the heads of cats.

The chancel has a heavy apex ceiling of a much later period than the nave ceiling; it was probably rebuilt when the chancel was reroofed with slates. I did admire the pulpit, in memory of the vicar the Rev. E.C.F. Jenkins, which was added in 1880 when many repairs were carried out. Four stone arches line the nave on either side, with plain wooden box-bench pews. The clerestories along the nave allow ample light into the church which is reflected off the white walls, making the interior bright inside. The west end of the nave has a stone door arch leading to the bell-ringers' chamber. Above the arch are three 18th-century commandment boards, one with the Lord's Prayer, another with the Creed, and between them are the Ten Commandments. Below them is a royal coat of arms, of George III.

The porch is on the south aisle which looks older than the rest of the church, with a Norman arch at the entrance. A lasting reminder of the church as I stood next to the pulpit, was the exquisite wooden carved choir stalls, accompanied by the organ. The bright sunshine shining through the windows and reflected off the walls transformed the chancel and stained-glass window above the altar into an angelic scene.

There is a memorial plaque in the church to Bernard Samuel Gilbert. He was born in Billinghay in 1882, the son of a seeds merchant of the town, and educated in Cambridge. His passion was writing, which he took seriously – so much so that he sold the family business and devoted his life to writing. Many of his works were written in the Lincolnshire dialect including poetry, plays and novels, which

Commandment boards in the Church of St Michael, Billinghay

were published. Some of his greatest work was poetry relating to the First World War; he died age 42 in 1927.

White's 1882 mentions 'Anthony Cressey Gilbert as being a seed, manure merchant and farmer'. He also mentions 'Edward Gilbert being a boat owner'. This may indicate that trade still came along the Billinghay Skirth Drain, in a period when rail transport was taking over from barge transport. The church has a warm feeling when you enter, being an open and welcoming house of God.

WALCOTT

Leaving Billinghay, still on the ridge I drove through the village of Walcott. *White's 1882* states that 'it is seated on a bold ridge near the Car Dyke navigation'; also that 'a large extent of fen land was enclosed in 1799, and now well drained and cultivated'.

CHURCH OF ST OSWALD

This small church, one of the Car Dyke Group of Parishes, stands just off the road. I say small, which it is, consisting of nave, chancel and south porch, with a bellcote on the west end of the nave. White states 'an ancient chapel of ease, St Oswalds went to decay about 1776 but a small new one was built in 1852 by subscription.

The village still has The Plough inn. I have to mention the inns in these villages because they are becoming a rarity and recording them will illustrate to future generations what we still had at this time in history. Apart from that, I love to frequent them. Inns have been the social hub of the countryside for centuries, especially in villages: somewhere to celebrate and commiserate with friends, neighbours and acquaintances, and even to meet the odd visitor such as myself.

The day I made my visit was a Wednesday, when coffee was being served in the church. Several people were there enjoying their coffee and biscuits, laughter replacing the chime of the single bell on the church. It was a happy group, who were keen to tell me the history of their wonderful place of worship. They showed me a stone that had come from nearby Catley Priory, on the floor between the wooden lectern and pulpit. The site of the priory is west of the village on the Digby road, although today only the earthworks remain. Peter de Billinghay founded it in the 12th century for the Gilbertine order of Sempringham, which was dissolved at the Reformation. While at Walcott I went down the fen road where I found the Car Dyke, with water trickling along it.

THORPE TILNEY

I really should have been looking for signs of the Car Dyke, so just north of Walcott I turned down the fen road at Thorpe Tilney hoping to find some signs of it. As the road descends I soon came to a sharp right-hand bend in the road, which on my OS Explorer map is on the 5 metre contour line, and sure enough there was the Car Dyke. That was in Thorpe Tilney Fen, supporting my thoughts on fen villages having a fen of their own. It was always said that the highlanders – those above the 5 metre contour line out of the fen – looked down on the fen people, but it was they who claimed the fen and gave it their village name.

The Car Dyke in Walcott Fen

If it was the Romans who built the Car Dyke, they followed the 5 metre contour line to almost every bend and curve from Billinghay along the rest of its course to Lincoln. It is as if they had used our present OS maps to plan its route.

Returning to Thorpe Tilney, heading north was a fine period house standing back off the road. It was, I found out later, Thorpe Tilney Hall, a Grade II listed building which must have been built in the 18th century. The building was of red brick with ashlar dressings, with slate roof and brick coped gables, with four very prominent brick gable chimneystacks. There was a very nice beech hedge along the road in front of the Hall which prevented me taking a photo, but maybe that is why it was there?

Once again my eyes focused on the soils in the fields, our lifeline for the future and always in my field of vision. Along this ridge of high land jutting into the fen I noticed the soils were of a mineral content, almost heathland, and yet either side of me, and not too far away, lay organic fen soils, all within a few miles of each other. It is fascinating to see how time has formed this mosaic of particles we call topsoil.

The Car Dyke in Thorpe Tilney Fen

TIMBERLAND

As I drove into Timberland village I saw a sign for the Anwick herd of Lincoln Red cattle, made famous by the late Mr Lol Bembridge. He devoted his entire working life to this iconic breed of the county. Many of the old English breeds of cattle owe their survival to the likes of breeders like Lol Bembridge. Not only were the family renowned breeders of Lincoln Red cattle but they were also great agriculturalists, devoted to the farming industry. Like many other Lincolnshire farmers, my own family had Lincoln Red cattle many years ago, and my father would take me to the annual Lincoln Red bull sales at Louth market. I was told Lol Bembridge had an emblem on his grass-field gates, and sure enough I found one of a Lincoln Red.

CHURCH OF ST ANDREW

One of the Car Dyke Group of Parishes, the church consists of a sturdy stone tower supported by four substantial buttresses. On each corner of the embattled tower are four ornate tapering pinnacles with four belfry windows and a clock on the west side.

The tall nave has stone mullion clerestories, north and south aisles having similar windows, the porch being on the south aisle. The chancel has a vestry on the north side and an interesting priest's door on the south side. It is an ancient wooden, heavily reinforced door with vertical uprights topped with geometrical tracery of the Early English period above it, sadly lacking in maintenance. White refers to the north aisle being rebuilt in 1792 and the chancel in 1838. Noticeable is the brick-work at the footings of the chancel and the upper part of the nave on the east end. The large crucifix surmounted on a stone base standing to greet you to this church is a monument to Christopher George Wheat, who was parish priest between 1878 and 1901. Of all the churches I have visited on my journey, to me this one looked most strong and solid, and maybe a reminder of the period of the yeoman farmer.

White's 1882 mentions £200 being paid from 'The Queen Ann's Bounty' for the purchase of land for the Glebe in Timberland parish. Queen Ann's Bounty was established in 1704 for the purchase of land to augment the incomes of the poorer clergy of the Church of England. It functioned until 1947 when assets were merged with the Ecclesiastical Commissioner, later known as the Church Commissioners. I have come across several land sales where small parcels of land in the fens as late as the 1920s were subject to a rent paid to Queen Ann's Bounty.

Queen Ann, daughter of James II, was Queen of England and Scotland in 1702 before the Union of Great Britain in 1707. She was a staunch Protestant and died in 1727.

It is interesting to compare *White's 1882* statistics with seating capacities of the various houses of worship in Timberland: 'C of E Church of St Andrew 200 persons, Non Conformist Chapels 360 persons, not including the Wesleyan Chapel in the Timberland Dales'. This was a period in history when the non-conformist religions had a great following, especially in the fens and along the fen-edge. The Wesleyan and Primitive Methodist chapels still survive as private residences.

Church of St Andrew: monument to the Rev. George Wheat who was the parish priest between 1878 and 1901

White also mentions that Lord Houghton was lord of the manor here, with a large estate along with that of Sir T. Whichcote. He says that a Court of foresters meet at The Houghton Arms inn and has 130 members and a fund of £573.14s. There is, however, very little commercial forestry around the district to be seen today, only the occasional remains of ancient forest. The Houghton Arms is now a private house. The Penny Farthing inn has survived in the village. *White's 1882* mentions a good school built in 1843 for 60 children on which are the coat of arms of the Whichcote family.

Leaving the village I drove down the fen road and crossed the Car Dyke on a bend in the road, still serving a useful purpose as a water carrier. The Car Dyke at this point is close to the village but then turns down towards the fen for a short distance before turning again to follow the line of the fen-edge alongside a wood. Blaeu's map of Timberland, dated 1645, shows Timberland Warfe on the line of the Car Dyke. The wooded area looked like ancient woodland and in the fen I noticed an embanked drain, a high water carrier which is the Timberland Delph.

Car Dyke alongside Timberland Fen

White's 1882, in his village comments on this part of the fen, mentions several times the 'Car Dyke navigation'. My instinct is that it was cut primarily as a navigable drain with an ample supply of catchwater coming off the higher ground west of the fen. It certainly had many watercourses feeding into it on its way from Peterborough to Lincoln, to enable many levels of water to be maintained for navigation purposes.

There are many names and terms for drainage channels across the fens. Delphs are found mainly in the upper Witham fens north of Billinghay; the word is derived from early English or Saxon origin. The north Lincolnshire fens have Branston, Nocton, Metheringham and Timberland Delphs cutting across their respective fens. These same delphs on Blaeu's map are listed as 'delves' not 'delphs'. The Lincolnshire west and east fens do not have any delphs as drainage channels.

As I drove through Timberland Fen I came across a sign which gave details of a Lancaster that had crashed in one of the fen fields. The plane had completed a bombing raid over Berlin on the 15th of February 1944, returning safely to Metheringham airfield. Whilst in the circuit waiting to land it collided with another aircraft also in the circuit, and as a result four of its crew were killed and three survived. It was a sad end after a successful raid, but touching that someone has remembered where they fell and marked the spot. During the Second World War this part of Lincolnshire was covered with airfields operated by Bomber Command. The skies were full of aircraft day and night and the drone of engines was constant, both for training and operations; sadly more left the Lincolnshire airfields than returned. We hold those brave men in our thoughts.

MARTIN

The village of Martin was my next port of call. Hissey's book *Over Fen and Wold,* published in 1889, mentions that he passed through Martin and he remarked how unsightly the house of worship was.

The church I saw was built some 20 odd years before he visited the village and was a fine building. He did travel through Martin Fen and described it as 'almost treeless, and hedge less, and wholly wanting the wild, weird beauty of the wider

The Church of St Michael at Martin

fenland, with its magic of colour and mystery of distance'. He was caught in a massive rainstorm in the middle of the fen, and 'was of the opinion that you can get as wet on an exposed fenland as anywhere'. He expected to cross 'the sloth-ful river Witham' on a ferry but the ferry had gone, replaced by a swing bridge, 'leaving the dreary fens without regret'.

CHURCH OF ST MICHAEL

I found the church of St Michael, one of the Car Dyke Group of Parishes, a stone structure, neat and well kept. It is in fact an ancient structure, which was refurbished in the 19th century. It consists of nave and chancel with vestries on

127

the north and south sides of the nave. Thatch was removed from the roof and replaced in 1869 with slate. *Kellys 1922* mentions that the tower was built in 1911. The tower is on the south side of the nave on the west end. A pyramidal cap surrounded by embattled stonework is on the top of the tower, with gargoyles on each corner of the tower under the battlements.

The church was locked on my visit so I could not see if there were aisles under the same roof-line as the nave. The porch has fine doors painted deep red, in an Early English plain arch. It is an attractive church in the centre of the village near the school. The entrance to the church is through some excellent wrought-iron gates and railings, though in need of some paintwork to bring them up to the pristine appearance of the church. The village has not been overdeveloped with residential or industrial properties and still has The Royal Oak inn.

MARTIN FEN

I decided to cross Martin Fen. I was told that the road across the fen was once a causeway leading over to Martin Dales. After the Second World War, aerial photographic surveys were carried out by the military, and many revealed causeways and settlements from the Roman occupation and even earlier. This was before deep cultivation was being used by farmers, and crop marks were easily identifiable from the air; now modern agricultural methods have obliterated such marks. Many early settlements were identified from those photographs and excavations and research were carried out by organisations such as the Heritage Trust of Lincolnshire with the help of local volunteers.

Remembering Hissey's comments, while in the middle of Martin Fen I wrote a few words:

> I gazed across that open plain
> Where fen blends into the sky
> With only me between them both
> Where spirits linger, rest and lie
> Solitude and mystery, I found it there
> Silence also, comes for free
> Clouds clear the mind of doubts and ills
> A heaven on earth, a place for me.

The word 'dale' in this region seems to be unique to settlements that have grown up along or near the River Witham, and not found in other parts of the fens. They are low-lying lands that have been reclaimed from flooding and allotted to various owners, from the villages between Walcott and Blankney along the Lincoln Cliff.

Car Dyke alongside Martin Fen

Further into the fen I could see Tattershall Castle peering above the tree line and as I approached the Dales the remains of Kirksted Abbey over the other side of the River Witham caught my eye. The drive across this area of the fens is very different from much of the fens I have travelled through. It is almost like driving across an inland sea with no water, from the heath behind me to the wolds in the distance – a plain opened up from the earth encompassed by the sky.

Living across at the Dales in the past must have felt very isolated from the outside world. Travelling in the uplands, distance is defined by the rise of hills on the horizon, while in the fens, distance can seldom be defined because the fen blends into the sky on the horizon, causing an illusion. Indeed, many times the illusion is a range of hills often with snow-capped peaks, which are in fact clouds.

After leaving Martin Dales to travel back across the fen, I turned left into Blankney Fen. I followed the Dales Head Dike and came across a machine 'mud-ding out' the dike. Many people had never heard of 'mudding out' until the disastrous floods in the Somerset Levels in 2013/14 when a lack of mudding out on the River Parrett was blamed for the flooding which took place. It's a controversy I will not get drawn into, my only comment being that advocates of 'not mud-ding out' did not suffer the devastation caused by the flooding. When I was seven I witnessed the catastrophic floods of 1947 in the fens, an event that will stay in my memory forever.

The machine I saw mudding out on the Dales Head Drain belonged to the Witham 1st Internal Drainage Board (IDB). As can be seen in the photo opposite, the extraction of mud from the drain along the entire length increases the water-holding capacity considerably.

The delphs which cross these fens are managed by the EA, as is the Car Dyke north of Billinghay, and the River Witham. Internal dykes, and drains below the 5 metre contour line are managed by Witham 1st IDB. There's not much to see in Blankney Fen except one or two isolated farmsteads near Blankney Dales, or a farmer busy on the land. A little tranquillity suits me in this modern age.

As I approached the fen-edge I could see an imposing farmhouse set just off the fen. I thought what an idyllic spot for a house, looking down on the Car Dyke, which runs just below it, the fen in the distance and the cliff behind. It is called Car Dyke Farm.

I drove down a concrete road running along the Car Dyke, a lovely drive with Blankney Woods on one side and open fen on the other. In the distance was the old sugar beet factory at Bardney. A sign on the roadside said it was a gated road and the gate may be locked, a fact confirmed by a lady who lives at the side of the Car Dyke in a secluded cottage. It was one of the most scenic parts of my journey along the fen-edge. The Car Dyke is most attractive here, which made me recollect Rawnsley's words which I quoted earlier on my journey, where he said that from Washingborough to Martin south of Lincoln, the Car Dyke was difficult to trace. What I was finding was very different: there are two Sites of National Conservation Interest north of the village of Martin: TF118617-TF121615 NW, Car-Dyke Farm and TF121614-TF122612, southeast of the farm itself.

Witham 4th IDB machine mudding out a fen drain

Rawnsley's journey was made almost a century ago and plenty has changed since then, but I sometimes wonder if he did actually visit all the places he wrote about, though that I will never know. This road took me into the fen and to my luck the gate was open. After a short distance I came back to the Car Dyke and on to Dunston village.

The soil was light and sandy with old-established woodlands nearby; one I passed near Dunston, looked like ancient woodland.

METHERINGHAM

As I drove from Dunston towards Metheringham the soil was light, what I call heathland. It was February and sugar beet was being lifted, the land ploughed and drilled. I mention this because much of the sugar beet is grown on heavier soils and it can be difficult to lift, and then to cultivate the soil for the following crop at this time of year. Just off the ridge to the west of the road the fenland petered out; it was the end of this strip stretching from South Kyme to the north of Martin.

REFLECTIONS

The Lincoln Cliff and the Car Dyke at its foot define the fen from here north to Washingborough. The Lincoln Cliff is the portion of a major escarpment that runs north–south through central Lincolnshire. The scarp is formed of Middle Jurassic rocks, principally the Lincolnshire Limestone series. It runs for over 50 miles from the Leicestershire border near Grantham to the River Humber, and is broken only twice by river gaps at Ancaster and Lincoln, through which the Rivers Slea and Witham respectively flow.

METHERINGHAM

Hissey had been to Dunston Pillar and travelled across the heath to Metheringham which he describes as 'an out-of-the-world, forsaken-looking little town; so out of the world, that I do not find it even in my Paterson, and why, or how, it exists at all was a puzzle to us … in times past it was shut away from the world, more than now by the wild extensive Lincolnshire heath on the one side and a narrow, though long, stretch of road-less fenland on the other, so was not very get-at-able … we baited our horses at a little inn here and whilst they were resting took a stroll around the place to see if we could find anything of interest, but we failed.' He mentions a cross in the village with disdain, but complimented the church with its Gothic arches supported by classic pillars, an architectural incongruity.

The centre of the village is still the hub for the community, with the Star & Garter inn, the community library, shops and café and the cross that Hissey mentions.

The village cross in front of the Star & Garter inn, Metheringham

In fact there is a new cross in the centre, as well as the old cross near the very neat, well-kept war memorial area. I was not sure what the old cross, rather a stump, had been used for. A lady told me it was an old water pump, but she was not sure if that was correct as she was a newcomer to the village. As I stood looking at it, a man asked me what I was doing, so I asked him if it was a pump or a cross. 'I don't know', he answered, 'I have lived here since the last war but came from Germany'. He said he was taken prisoner by the Americans on the Dutch-German border and sent to America as a POW. After the war he was sent to England to work on the land in Lincolnshire where he remains to this day. He settled here and married an English girl, working for an agricultural spraying contractor in this village. Eventually he became the general manager of that company. He seemed to know everyone who passed by and exchanged greetings with them, but was of no help on the old stone stump – but life is about people. *White's 1882* mentions an ancient cross that stood in the village and was replaced in 1835 where a market was held on Saturday evenings. That 1835 cross was demolished by an American forces lorry during the Second World War and was not replaced until the millennium.

CHURCH OF ST WILFRED

The square tower is embattled, of Decorated English style, with two clocks and windows in the belfry. The nave is embattled with clerestories, north and south aisles with transepts on the tower, chancel with vestry. *White's 1882* mentions the church having extensive restoration carried out on the chancel and the north aisle in 1858 and 1870. It is a handsome church near the centre of the village, and well kept. It was however locked, so I could not see inside.

The war memorial, Metheringham

REFLECTIONS

Unlike Hissey, I liked the village and its people, who were charming and friendly. I went into the small village library and remarked how nice it was to see a library still open in a village when so many had closed. The reason was that they were all helpful friendly volunteers, upholding a community spirit. Many country villages have witnessed an influx of people from other places. I believe it is partly they who have transformed and integrated with local people and who wish to belong to a community again, which they probably did not do in the cities they left.

After leaving Metheringham I felt the impulse to travel over the heath following Hissey's journey to see Dunston Pillar. The pillar was erected in 1751 by Francis Dashwood Esq. to guide travellers across the heath at night, having a lighted beacon on its summit. After the heath was enclosed, a statue of George III was erected on it. It became a danger to low-flying aircraft from nearby RAF airfields and so was reduced in height and the statue removed, part of which remains in Lincoln Museum.

Metheringham Heath is a place for solitude, an area of wide open countryside with few farmsteads or houses. Halfway across the heath I was getting bored so I cut across to Dunston Heath.

Hissey had stopped at the pillar and wondered what it was, so he asked a man who was standing nearby.

'That ? Oh , that's Dunston Pillar', he replied. 'You can see it for miles around in almost every direction ... it used to be a lighthouse.'

'What, a lighthouse so far inland?' Hissey exclaimed.

'Yes' said the man.

Hissey's remark was that 'a lighthouse could be useful inland as well as at sea'. When he crossed the heath it would have been a barren landscape, and probably much of it not farmed during that period of agricultural recession. Now it is well farmed, thanks to modern husbandry, with hedges lining the roads and woods on the higher ground. What I did find unsettling, even in this unpopulated area, was the lack of vision, which was obstructed by tall hedges as I drove along the roads. It was as if I was enclosed on the road with nothing to see on either side of me but hedges; for miles I could not even see a crop. Before the enclosures it was open countryside, then enclosed by hedges after the enclosures. Even if the pillar was restored to its original height, today it would not be able to guide travellers across the heath. The transformation of woods on the highest part of the heath would obstruct their view of the pillar. Maybe it was my love of the open fenland, after seeing Dunston Pillar, which drew me back across Dunston Heath to the village of Dunston.

DUNSTON

The houses in Dunston village are a mix of stone and brick, with the church of St Peter in the centre of the village. I parked near The Red Lion inn and

Dunston Beck running through Dunston village

walked along to the green where Dunston Beck runs through the village; I was fascinated by where it comes from and where it is going, always on the move. It was coming from Dunston Heath, crystal-clear and at a steady flow; through the water I could see the stones on the bed of the beck. The quality of many of our water carriers has improved considerably over the past decades, due mainly to water directives from the European Union.

The beck was flowing down to Nocton Wood where it joins the Car Dyke and then leaves to flow down Nocton Delph across the fen. Not hurrying, but trickling along heading for the River Witham and eventually blending into saline waters when it reaches the Wash. How is it that such pure, crystal-clear water from the heathlands with an identity, travels to become nothing more than a particle in our saline oceans?

THE RIVER

Why hurry little river
Why hurry to the sea
There is nothing there to do
But to sink into the blue
But the tides for evermore
And the faint and far off line
Where the winds cross the brine
For ever ever roam
And never find a home

Fredrick George Scott 1861–1944, poet, author and Anglican priest

CHURCH OF ST PETER

The Marquis of Ripon rebuilt the main body of the church in 1875; the tower being earlier was retained. There is a nave, which has a large chancel on the east end, north and south aisles, with the porch on the south aisle. The tower is em-battled with pinnacles on four corners, a clock on the south side, and contains five bells.

The interior of the church is very light considering it has no clerestories in the nave, the light coming from the large aisle and chancel mullioned windows. I rather liked the pews, or should I say benches, with their ornate carved ends and an attractive stone and wooden pulpit. The chancel is also attractive with the choir stalls and organ under a stone arch, all for the benefit of the local community.

As I left the village I noticed the old vicarage, a large house with outbuildings which has been developed. The parish of Dunston extends east to the River Witham and west to Dunston Pillar on Lincoln Heath, on the A15 just south of Waddington Airfield, four miles west of the village. Almost all the villages and towns on my journey along the fen have a portion of fen in their parishes. Dunston has fen as well as heathlands.

The villages of Blankney, Metheringham, Nocton and Potterhanworth all include fen and heath. Branston, on the edge of the heath, has both fen and heathland in its parish.

Seeing a sign to the fen road, I travelled down it and was surprised to see so much old woodland on my left, a transformation from the heath to the west and the open fen in the east. The road followed the wood round to the left, with Dunston Beck feeding into an old watercourse on the edge of the wood, which was the Car Dyke.

The wood is Nocton Wood and where I parked was a small conservation area with an information board. The road beside the wood was an unmade road but good to drive along so I carried on along the line of the wood and fen, past Nocton Delph and Wasps Nest to Abbey Hill. The Car Dyke is still evident there so I carried on towards Neville Wood and eventually to Potterhanworth. This whole area between Timberland and Potterhanworth is the most dramatic stretch I have found of fen, with parts of the Car Dyke almost unchanged since its creation. The contrast is clearly defined between upland and fen, only a short distance apart. It is worth exploring far more than I had time for on my journey that day, but it will draw me back again before too long.

Car Dyke at Wasps Nest along Nocton Fen

NOCTON

Having heard so much about the Nocton estate from my father, I decided to visit the village, it being on my list of fen-edge settlements. It has always been a renowned agricultural estate, having changed owners many times. It was once owned by a farmer from Cornwall who grew daffodils there on the light soils. Smiths Potato Crisps farmed the estate back in the 1960s, and now the estate belongs to the Dyson family of vacuum cleaner fame. The estate was not only renowned for farming but also for its sporting amenities and I remember my father saying how good the pheasant shooting was there. The village and surrounding area owe their origins and splendour to such families as the Earls of Buckinghamshire and later the Marquis of Ripon who cherished their estates.

As I turned down into the village I had to stop to admire the church spire rising above the houses in the village. I don't know why, but such a view makes me think of England, a scene you always dream of when in a foreign land, and wish you were home. The village has many attractive stone houses and cottages, along with a lovely old school building, which appeared very active as I drove past it to the church. The church and the school were designed by Sir Gilbert Scott RA and built during the mid-19th century.

CHURCH OF ALL SAINTS

The tower is in two stages, surmounted with a tapering spire on the west end of the church and partly joining the nave on the north side. It is the tower and spire that dominate the church, giving it an elevated appearance above the nave and chancel. Walking through the entrance gates to the church one is welcomed to the porch at the base of the tower on the north side. On the south aisle of the church there is a second porch and a vestry on the east end of the aisle. The nave has clerestories, which consist of four windows set in a blind arcade.

The church was locked. As I drove out of the village, the old post office stood tall and upstanding in front of me, such a fine stone building built in 1833. Estates such as Nocton, and several more in this part of Lincolnshire, were the property of the landed gentry in the days before many estates were sold after the First World War. Invariably the owners lived on these estates and made sure the village houses, cottages and other amenities were fitting to their taste. It is to them we owe this fine legacy and the reason we have such quintessential English places today.

As I left the village I passed some fine old Wellingtonia trees behind a wall surrounding what was and is a large house. I love these trees as I mentioned when in Dunsby earlier on my journey. I did notice a very large housing development on the edge of the village; like many of our villages they will soon become as large as some of our towns. Will the day come when all the villages are joined together, and lose their identity, as perhaps another travel writer will record for future readers?

POTTERHANWORTH

Driving from Nocton to Potterhanworth, still on the cliff, the road climbs up into the village and the church greets you as you enter. As I parked near the church entrance I could not help but notice a red-brick building on the other side of the road, and I thought what an unusual building it was in the centre of a village. Walking over to it I soon realised it was, or had been, a water tower with a tank above the brickwork topped with a slate roof. It has three stone plaques on

The old water tower in Potterhanworth

141

which are coats of arms on a small tower, on top of which is a steel ladder up to a small entrance in the roof. It was in extremely good condition and well preserved and by its appearance it may have been converted to a private residence. *Kellys 1922* mentions a water tower, which contained 37,000 gallons of water pumped from an artesian well by wind and oil-powered engines from Damend Field. The tower also contains two rooms, one of which is used for meetings of the parish council and the men's institute. It definitely adds to the village's charm.

REFLECTIONS

White's 1842 refers to much of the soil belonging to Christ's Hospital Lincoln, but there is no mention of that in his 1882 directory.

Maybe the great agricultural depression, between 1870 and 1914, had taken its toll and forced another estate to be sold. It was a difficult time for estate owners across the country, but fortunes change frequently, and one person's dilemma can be the good fortune of others. Many tenant farmers during that period and in the depression of the 1920s were able to buy their holdings.

CHURCH OF ST ANDREW

The church was mostly rebuilt in 1749 and again in 1856 except the tower. The square tower on the west end of the nave has clock faces on all four sides. The top of the tower has a balustrade with retriculated tracery, and pinnacles on each corner decorated with crockets. Beneath each corner of the balustrade are dog-like gargoyles. Four stages of angle buttresses support the tower on the west end, which has a cut mark on the base of the tower. The tower is the oldest part of the church. The nave has an apex slate roof, a chancel on the east end with vestry on the north side, the entrance to the church being a porch on the north aisle at the west end. The north aisle has an apex roof with a gully between it and the nave roof, all roofing being slate. Inside, the nave and aisle ceilings are wooden arched-brace, the arches being semi-circular. Along the nave are plain wooden bench pews, with four stone arches lining the nave on either side, opening into

the aisles. The church was open for visitors and worshippers; it was warm, light, and had a welcoming aura about it. An added bonus was some excellent home-made ginger marmalade for sale, which I could not resist buying to take home.

Still on high ground, after leaving the village I passed through a wooded area on the Bardney road out to Potterhanworth Booths, the latter being only a cluster of houses. The word 'booth' describes a small temporary dwelling, probably where shepherds and stockmen lived during the summer months when tending their herds and flocks on the fens.

BRANSTON

Hissey visited Branston on his travels and described it thus: 'Branston we found to be all that it had been represented to us. A very pretty village indeed it was, composed chiefly of stone built cottages, pleasantly weathered-tinted, many having Picturesque porches, and nearly all possessing little flower gardens in front, gay with colour and sweet of odour. ... Branston would have done credit to Devonshire, a country of Picturesque villages; it was the kind that ladies love to term sweet and pretty.' He then went on to say, 'If it had been in Devonshire it would be painted, photographed, and written about, poets would have written about it, and visited by many people, but being in Lincolnshire out of the travelers beat, its charms are reserved for the favoured few whom chance may bring that way.' Having read of Hissey's visit and praises I felt I had to follow in his footsteps to see what it is like after a century and a quarter. Branston is a village that has many parts to its name. It has moorlands, which were quite common in the fens, being areas of deep peat. It has its own fen, Branston Fen, and its own island, Branston Island, on the east side of

This house was once the Old Bertie Arms, Branston

the River Witham. Branston Booths is a satellite settlement on the west side of the fen, and Branston Beck feeds into the Car Dyke and then into Branston Delph.

The village is situated on the cliff, but I would still include it as a fen-edge settlement, having so much association with its own fen assets. I saw a sign on the wall of a house in the village which read, 'In this Inn, known as The Bertie Arms, was held on the 26th May 1765 the inaugural meeting to institute the enclosure of the parish lands of Branston'.

The population of the parish in 1801 was 446 increasing to 1,431 in 1881. Like many other fen villages, its population increased when the fen commons were enclosed and drained in the late 18th and 19th centuries.

Workers moved to the parish as a result of the drained fenland, changing it from pastoral farming to mixed arable farming which required more labour.

The fen soils, which had been enclosed and drained, would have had a very high peat content. These high organic soils have low pH levels and a lime deficiency, requiring burnt lime to raise the levels in order to grow crops. The surrounding area being on a sub-strata of limestone was ideal for the extraction of lime; the many local lime-kilns fulfilled this requirement.

I wandered around the centre of the village and had to agree with Hissey: it has not lost its charm. Houses have been built since his visit, which tastefully blend in with the old surrounds. As in most villages development has happened, especially in the past four decades, but the area around the church he would find very similar to his visit. Near the church was the church hall, busy serving tea and cakes to local residents, and below the church is The Wagon and Horses looking spick and span. In the car park near the hall is a timeline mosaic depicting time at Branston; it was designed by Alan Potter and made by the Branston local history group. Incorporated in the mosaic are four Japanese cherry trees, their shining dark brown bark adding to the colour of the decorative design.

Left: *Branston: the timeline mosaic.* Centre: *Hainton Hall, former rectory, built by the Rev. Peregrine Curtois, patron and incumbent.* Right: *Church of All Saints, Branston: the nave and ceiling, restored after the fire in 1962*

Houses with names, which conjure up village life as it was a century ago, line the streets near the green, trades gone but not forgotten. Close to the church is Hainton Hall, a fine red-brick mansion now converted into flats. It was built by the Rev. Peregrine Curtois, BCL, who was patron and incumbent of the living here between 1768 and 1814. In 1920 a celebration took place to mark the 244th anniversary of the Curtois family's association with the parish of Branston.

CHURCH OF ALL SAINTS

The church stands in the old part of the village on a high mound, giving it a status of its own. It is of Norman and Early English styles, restored in 1876 by designs of Sir George Gilbert Scott. Hissey comments, 'The church too was aged, and gray, and we noticed in the walls some "long-and-short" work showing rude but lasting Saxon masonry and proving that a church was there before the Conquest … A bit of history told in stone … The hoary fane suggested an interesting interior, but we found the doors to be carefully locked and we felt in no humour to go a-clerk hunting.' For me too the church was locked when I made my visit, but to my good fortune the Rector, the Rev. Lora Brabin-Smith, and two churchwardens arrived and made me most welcome. I had noticed new windows in the chancel before they arrived and made a comment on them. I was told that on Boxing Day 1962 the organ had caught fire and destroyed most of the chancel and the ceiling. Luckily the fire was contained, otherwise the whole church would have been destroyed. The church structure has been restored to a very high standard and various items of church furniture replaced, making the church probably more beautiful than it was in Hissey's day. I was extremely pleased to have been able to see inside such a wonderful church.

There is a tower with a spire and a clock on the west end of the nave which has clerestories, a chancel, north and south aisles with a porch on the south aisle. Adjoining the north aisle is a vestry, which served as a girls' school for many years.

White mentions 'open benches with the ones along the nave with carved poppy heads, retained from the old pews'. Luckily these survived the fire and remain for future generations to sit on (www.branstonallsaints.co.uk).

The church has so much of interest for those fortunate enough to find it open as I did. I was sad to leave the village but felt that I must return to the fen and look for the Car Dyke again, so I headed downhill to Branston Booths.

BRANSTON BOOTHS

The Car Dyke can easily be identified at the Branston Delph sluice, but along the drive towards Washingborough only parts of it remain. These northern fens, Washingborough and Heighington Fens, are mainly pasture, grazed with sheep and cattle – no different to how they were farmed centuries ago. It brought back memories of when we had livestock on the farm, so much so that I carried on past Washingborough until the fen ran out. The Car Dyke must have passed here but I found no evidence of it remaining.

HEIGHINGTON

The village is, and has been for many centuries, in the parish of Washingborough and today it is practically one township. With the proposed future development proposals in the country it will become more urbanised. *White's 1882* mentions the village being on the banks of a rivulet, today called the Mill Stream. He also mentions The

The Turks Head inn, Heighington

Turk's Head inn which has survived to this day. The old part of the village is a mix of stone and brick houses, blending together to give it an attractive appearance.

CHURCH OF ST THOMAS

The church was transformed from a chapel of ease to its present form. Parts of the original tower were preserved and the chancel added in 1865. The north aisle is a separate addition and has a chimney for a fire inside the building. *White's 1882* mentions a school being built near the near the chapel at the same time as the church was rebuilt. The church was locked on my visit so I could not see inside, or see if this part of the church was indeed originally a school building.

Buttresses support the sturdy Gothic tower to the last stage which is embattled with an ornamental moulding around the top. On one corner is a large, ornate pinnacle giving the tower a unique appearance. The transformation from the chapel to the present church is visible in the stonework, but the geometrical tracery in the chancel windows is in keeping with the ancient tower.

WASHINGBOROUGH

At one time Washingborough was no more than a small village on the lower slopes of the Lincoln Cliff overlooking the fen. Being close to the city of Lincoln, expansion over the years has practically joined it with Heighington village. I would have thought in the present climate of house building further development will occur and the village will change again as it has done at times in the past. *White's 1882* quotes a population of 743; today it is over 3,000.

Situated on the banks of the River Witham, the Sincil Dike experienced barge traffic before the railway came through. This line is still in use, being the main line from Lincoln to Sleaford. Moorlands and fen commons were enclosed as late as 1834. Washingborough was said to be the site of the last fort to guard the Car Dyke before Lincoln, but I have found no evidence of this or indeed of other forts mentioned on the route.

White's 1882 mentions The Hunter's Leap and The Ferry Boat inns which have survived to this day; let us hope they will continue. The centre of the old part of the village stands on high ground with a small green on which there is an old cross, used as a memorial to the fallen in the two World Wars. When I visited the green

Washingborough village cross and war memorial

it was overshadowed by a large tree, and the cross was surrounded with wheelie bins, which have become part of our street furniture, necessary but often spoiling our street scenes, like motor vehicles. On my journey I have noticed the increase in vehicles parked along the streets, noticeable because I have found it impossible to take photographs of some street scenes. Most of our villages and towns were not built to accommodate the motor car, a hazard we have to put up with.

The stroll up to the church is still reminiscent of an old village with attractive houses on either side

CHURCH OF ST JOHN THE EVANGELIST

The Early English square tower standing erect on the cliff-edge towers above the village, the tower embattled with pinnacles on each corner. Four belfry windows permit the bells to ring out across the fen and moor, with a handsome clock on the east side of the tower. The nave has unusual clerestories on both north and south aisles with the porch on the south aisle. A large chancel extends from the nave with a vestry on the north side. The vestry has a chimney and I wondered if, like Branston Church, it may have been used as a school, but the church being locked I was not able to delve deeper.

My lasting memory of the church were the windows in both aisles. These display geometrical tracery, two to each aisle from the Early English period. Later these simple designs gave way to more elaborate and decorative designs during the Decorated English period. Another feature that caught my attention was the square holes on the top two sections of the tower. They must have had a purpose, be it only nesting holes for the jackdaws I saw entering and exiting them.

I was tempted to journey into the city of Lincoln, but my intention had been to explore the fen-edge, wherever that may be. I know the city and have visited it and stayed there many times during my lifetime, sometimes socially and at other times researching for my books. It is a wonderful city to explore; one could almost say it is two cities, the

The Ferry Boat inn, Washingborough

upper and the lower. I would certainly advocate visiting it if you have not been before. The city stands majestically above the cliff and the fens, with the heath and wolds in its sights, the pinnacle being its cathedral (www.visitlincoln.com).

Coming to my journey's end I wanted to view Lincoln Cathedral from the fen on the bank of the River Witham before I returned home. As I drove along the road towards Branston Booths I could find little if any sign of the Car Dyke. Passing the grasslands of Washingborough Fen it was pleasing to see a part of the fen not under the plough or the drill. I make that comment being an arable farmer myself and accept the fact that the fens had to be broken up from pasture for arable cropping to feed the public. Crossing Washingborough Fen I arrived at the bridge over the Sincil Drain which one can drive over and park your car.

The railway from Lincoln to Boston once ran along the riverside; it was closed long ago and is now a walking and cycle path. There was the odd car parked there and a friendly dog walker, but apart from that it was a place of solitude, with an excellent view of the cathedral. From here one can walk to Lincoln along the Viking Way or the opposite way to Bardney Lock, and further on if one wishes. I stood on the footbridge over the river and convinced myself that this was fen-edge country, an undefined part of England linked by two majestic cathedrals, Peterborough and Lincoln and the Roman Car Dyke.

It has convinced me that I must also explore further fen-edge country in other counties that claim individual parts of the fens.

A DAY ALONG THE DELPHS

After my journey, while reading up my notes, I received a call from Jake Reeds. Somehow word had reached the Environment Agency in Spalding that I was planning a journey which involved the Car Dyke, and that I had been enquiring about the delphs in the northern fens. Jake, the fishery officer for the EA, invited me for a trip out with him. He had work to carry out in that part of the fen, so he kindly took me from Spalding up across the Lincoln Heath to Potterhanworth.

A short distance after leaving the village the road drops into Potterhanworth Fen, passing The Plough inn on a corner. Jake soon pointed out the Car Dyke – not such a fine example as that between Martin and Nocton but still evident and now a small watercourse. We followed the Car Dyke along the road to Branston Booths where we stopped at Branston Delph sluice.

From the sluice we drove to the outfall of the delph down a hard road, once a concrete road. Many concrete roads were laid in the post Second World War years on unstable fen soils, to enable crops to be brought out of the fens during the winter months. They were not reinforced and have broken up, making them in some places impassable; it's the same in many of the Cambridgeshire fens. The journey back across the fen was rewarding, not just for the environment and tranquility, but also for the view of Lincoln Cathedral, visible up on the Lincoln Cliff and shrouded in the morning haze.

Branston Booths, showing the Car Dyke where it turns into the Branston Delph. Its course to Lincoln is in the foreground

Having arrived at the delph outfall, Jake showed me the sluice where the delph discharges into the Sincil Drain. The Sincil brings water from the centre of Lincoln city and then runs parallel to the River Witham before discharging into the river at Bardney Lock. This is a man-made dyke; its origin is uncertain but certainly pre-medieval and maybe even Roman. It was originally, and still is, a drainage channel which was extended by John Rennie in the 19th century from Stamps End to the Bardney Locks. I also saw a pile of bog oaks here that had been extracted from the peat soil.

We returned along the same broken concrete road back to Branston Booths and on to Potterhanworth to cross the Potterhanworth Fen. While travelling along that road I noticed a crop of carrots being grown, which we used to associate with fen peat soils. At one time in the fens, carrots were only grown on peat soils where the soil was piled up over the crop to protect it from frosts in the winter months. Chatteris, near Ely on the black fen soils, was the capital of carrot growing in the fens, but now no longer. The growing of carrots has moved to lighter soils out of the fens, brought about by changing demands for the crop, especially for pre-packed carrots, as well as by the changes in growing and harvesting methods.

The drive across the fen was over wide-open countryside, giving one a feeling of space and freedom. It is on the line of an ancient causeway across the fen such as the one I travelled on previously across Martin Fen.

As we travelled along the road I could see the old Bardney sugar beet factory in front of me. The soil here was darker, slightly organic and I noticed a large covered heap of maize in a field. This is a crop that has witnessed a large increase in acreage in the past few years. It is grown, stored in sealed heaps, then eventually used to fuel the anaerobic digester plants that generate gas to drive turbines producing electricity. Many people will have noticed these digester plants around the countryside – they look like space stations with a domed roof.

Jake told me about the Bardney Lock on the River Witham, and Branston Island close by. The island is between the present River Witham and the Old River Witham, in the parish of Branston. Before we came to the river we turned off left down a farm track – no one seemed to mind it being used to get to the lock.

The lock was fascinating, with not many craft passing through in February, but I am told it is very busy in the more clement months of the year. It was a tranquil spot with only the odd cyclist along the old railway and hardy fishermen near the lock. Jake informed me that the fish seem to congregate near the places where there is human habitation, maybe being safer there from four-legged predators in the watercourses. His work involves monitoring fish numbers and the welfare of fish stocks over a very wide area of the east of England.

Left: *The Car Dyke at Timberland Delph sluice.* Right: *Bardney Lock on the River Witham: the Barlingtons Eau (the old River Witham) on the left discharging into the River Witham on the right*

Artificial spawning beds for fish in the River Witham

I say work, but to me it seemed more of a pleasure than a chore to him, and so heartwarming for me to see the kind of people we are relying on to preserve our countryside. I believe many of the younger generation – younger than me, that is – wish to preserve our countryside far more than my generation did. However, one must remember that my generation, and the previous one, had to produce food at any cost during wartime and the post-war years. This was at a time when agrochemicals were being used without enough research into their consequences to nature and humans alike. Meadows, pastures, woodlands, moorland, heath, wold and fen had to be turned over to food production whatever the costs. Wars change people and places.

We made our way back on the fen side of the Witham, where Jake pointed out what were, many years ago, flood washes running alongside the river at the bottom of Nocton and Metheringham Fens. We also went to a house in the middle of the fen where an old wind pump once stood, a secluded spot to live, but not for me in the winter. It was so remote I don't think I could find it again.

We found our way to Martin where we slipped along the Car Dyke to the sluice at Timberland Delph. The sun was shining and as we got out of our vehicle to look along the delph, a flash of colour caught our eye: a kingfisher streaking off along the water under the trees. I love this time of the year for taking photos, when the trees are bare, wildlife is easy to see and one can follow lines of flight, especially of the elusive kingfisher.

He was however too fast for me to photograph.

The delph at this end of the fen is very overgrown with little water to sustain fish and other water species; it's ideal for the reed-nesting birds but that is all. I am not an expert on this subject but it does seem to me we are lacking in regular maintenance of some of our watercourses managed by the EA. If carried out it could eliminate some flooding and enrich the watercourses for fish, birds and other wildlife.

Later in the day we drove across Timberland Fen to the Timberland Delph outfall which discharges into the River Witham.

I love standing on these outfalls watching waters come off the cliff, down through the fen to join the flow of other waters in the Witham and off to the sea. It has taken generations of planning by engineers and board members to perfect this management of water flows, in harmony with mother nature. It was lunch-time and having some lunch with us we unpacked our sandwiches and ate them while standing at the delph sluice – no finer setting for a break in our journey.

Timberland Delph sluice on the River Witham, our venue for lunch

GLOSSARY

Beck A stream of highland water (as distinguished from a fen drain).

Black fen Soil with a high organic content, giving the appearance of being black or dark brown.

Booth Temporary dwelling or hamlet; probably borrowed from Old Scandinavian/Old Danish *both* = booth, stall.

Broach [spire] A spire which surmounts an unparapeted tower joined together by masonry.

Carr Low-lying fen woodland, mostly brush.

Chain A measure of distance equal to 22 yards. Used in the past in agriculture and drainage activities.

Clerestories Windows in the walls of the nave, between the aisle roof and the nave roof, allowing in light to the nave.

Counter A drain running parallel with a main drain or river.

Corbel A short block of stone or timber which projects from a wall to support a beam, an arch or any horizontal feature.

Corbel table Row of exterior or interior corbels supporting a roof, parapet, broach spire or cornice, usually connected.

Crockets Projecting buds, flowers, curled leaves or bunches of foliage usually carved and placed at regular intervals along the sides of arches, canopies, spires, finials, pinnacles, gables, etc.

Cut mark Often found on churches and prominent structures, reference to height above sea level. Later referring to spot and trig points.

Dales Low-lying lands near a river, in the fens only found along the River Witham.

Delph A Saxon word for ditch, frequently applied to a drain running parallel with and at the foot of a bank.

Devil's door A door on the north side of a church. Legend has it that they were left open at baptisms to allow the child's evil spirits to leave; they were also used for processions at the same service, and at funerals.

Drove A track or road mainly used for driving livestock along.

Duck decoy A pond for catching live ducks.

Dyke, dike The ancient English term for a bank protecting land from the inundations of water from the sea, or from a watercourse. Over time both bank and the hollow ground cut to form a bank became known as a dyke. Dugdale, like dyke, applies to both bank and hollows. Today a dyke is a man-made drainage channel.

EA Environment Agency

Eau A drain; from the Scandinavian *aa* = water.

Finial Leaf-like decoration which forms the terminal at the top of a gable, canopy, bench-end, tower, corner etc.

Gate Nordic for road.

Hagioscope A hole in a wall or pillar between an aisle and the chancel so that the main altar can be seen through it; also know as a squint.

IDB Internal drainage boards.

Intercommoning Commons shared by several villages.

Lode Fenland drainage channel used for navigation, often banked.

Mere A fen lake.

Mineral soils Soils containing sand, stone or gravel.

Moor Area in the fen consisting of deep peat, remnants of ancient decomposed woodlands.

ODN Ordnance Datum Newyln; the datum at Newyln Cornwall for measurements above sea level.

Parvis A room over a porch, often used as a schoolroom.

Piscina Niche containing a bowl or drain, usually built into the wall of the chancel near the altar.

Rood screen Carved wooden or stone screen which divides the nave from the choir and chancel.

Saltern Site where salt was extracted from the sea water. Evidence of Iron Age and Romano-British sites are found in the fens.

Sedilia Set of seats recessed in niches in the south wall of the chancel, used by the priest and his assistants.

Skirt Edge.

Spandrel The space between the curve of an arch of a door and the enclosing mouldings.

SSSI Site of Special Scientific Interest.

Triforium Blank arcading gallery or walled passage between the top of the main arcade and the clerestory above.

Turves Blocks of peat cut and dried for fuel.

Tympanum Space between the lintel above a door and the arch shape above it; characteristic of Norman and Gothic buildings.

Voussior Forms the arch leading up to the keystone on a bridge.

Wash Area embanked alongside a river which allows excess floodwaters to be released later back into the river.

BIBLIOGRAPHY

Trevor A. Bevis, *A Guide to the Fens and Fenland Churches*, 1971 edition

Mark Child, *Church Architecture*, 1976

J. Charles Cox & Alfred Harvey, *English Church Furniture*, first edition 1907

William Dugdale, *The History of Imbanking and Draining of Divers Fens & Marshes both in Foreign Parts and in this Kingdom*, second edition 1722

Fenland Notes & Queries, Volume 6, 1904–06

E. Gervoise, *The Ancient Bridges of Mid and Eastern England*, 1932

Hillary Healey, *A Fenland Landscape Glossary for Lincolnshire*, 1997

Heritage Trust of Lincolnshire, Brian Simmons and Paul Cope-Faulkner, *The Car Dyke Lincolnshire Archaeology and Heritage Report Series No 8*, 2006

James John Hissey, *Over Fen & Wold*, 1898

Kellys Directory of Lincolnshire, 1922

Samuel H. Miller, *Handbook of the Fenland*, 1889

Samuel H. Miller and Skertchly, *Fenland Past and Present*, 1878

W.J. Rawnsley, *The Highways and Byways of Lincolnshire*, 1914, pocket edition 1926

W.H. Wheeler, *The History of the South Lincolnshire Fens*, 1868

White's Directory of Lincolnshire, 1842, 1882

INDEX

ACKNOWLEDGEMENTS

Researching my last three books was a great challenge in many respects, this book being a very different experience. Exploring has always been a great passion of mine, especially my homeland, the fens. Stepping out of the fens along the fen-edge has been an interesting experience, not as challenging as researching, more of a joyful pastime. The challenge has been turning my exploits into this book with the help of my copyeditor Katherine James along with Megan Sheer who designed the cover, and carried out the print setting.

I thank them both for their work, patience with me, and helping me to prepare this book. I am sure at times they must have thought I had just risen out of one of the fen bogs along with the bog-oaks.

I wish to thank Jellyfish Solutions for printing, marketing and distributing my book, and Maggie our help in the house for keeping my office tidy between breaks in my work.

I must not forget my wife Steph who has always helped, encouraged and assisted me through busy periods on the farm, and my Border terrier Peanut, who has often dragged me from my desk for walks to clear the mind.